W9-AGR-345

Library Form 10

Date Due

MAR 1 2 '65	MAY 5 '67	OCT 21 71	
	JUL 1 '68		
MAR 26 '65	MAR 2 6 '69		
Apr5			
APR 1 2 '65	MAR 2 5 '71		
MAY 2 '65	APR 28 71		
MAY 14	MAY 1 3 71		
	DEC 1 3 71		
MAY 28 '65	MAY 2 6 '72		
OCT 1 5 '65	DEC 1 4 72		
NOV 5 '65	DEC 2 2 '72		
	APR 1 2 1973		
NOV 2 4 '65			
APR 1 5 '66	MAY 2 2 73		
JUN 1 '66			
MAR 2 4 '67			
APR 1 0 '67			
APR 2 4 '67			
NOV 1 4 '67			

*The
United States
in
the Korean
War*

THE UNITED STATES
IN THE KOREAN WAR

Illustrated
with
photographs,
and maps
by
Robert Standley

DON LAWSON

Defending
Freedom's
Frontier

Abelard-Schuman
London
New York
Toronto

Cobb School Library
JEFFERSON ELEM. SCHOOL LIBRARY
DULUTH, MINNESOTA

© Copyright 1964 by Don Lawson
Library of Congress Catalogue
Card Number: 64-13152

LONDON

Abelard-Schuman
Limited
8 King Street WC2

NEW YORK

Abelard-Schuman
Limited
6 West 57th Street

TORONTO

Abelard-Schuman
Canada Limited
896 Queen Street W.

Printed in the United States of America
Designed by The Etheredges

To Toppy,
Without Whose Early
and Continued
Encouragement
None
of My Books
Would Have Been
Written

Acknowledgments

The author wishes to express his thanks to Wayne M. Hartwell, Librarian, F. E. Compton & Co., for his assistance in research and in the preparation of the bibliography. Thanks are also due to Verne Pore for preparing the index, Bernard Holliday for his work on the photographs, and Eleanor Brooks for typing the final manuscript.

Tony March, Editor of the Army *Times,* was most helpful in supplying information about Medal of Honor winners in Korea. Particular thanks are also due to Alice R. Martin of the Air Force Book Program for her assistance in obtaining photographs from the several branches of the Armed Forces, the Air Force, Army, Navy and Marines. The individual service branches were also most cooperative in this regard.

Finally, the author wishes to express his great appreciation to the following publishers for permitting him to use material from books on their lists:

Holt, Rinehart and Winston, Inc. *The Last Parallel* by Martin Russ.

Alfred A. Knopf, Inc. *MacArthur: His Rendezvous with History* by Courtney Whitney.

G. P. Putnam's Sons. *Conflict: the History of the Korean War* by Robert Leckie. Copyright 1962 by Robert Leckie.

The Viking Press. *General Dean's Story* by William F. Dean.

Harper & Row, Inc. *From the Danube to the Yalu* by Mark W. Clark, *The New Breed* by Andrew C. Geer and *Reactionary!* by Lloyd W. Pate.

Contents

- *Korean Chronology*   *11-14*
- *List of Illustrations*   *15-16*

One   •   *The Capture of General Dean*   *19*

Two   •   *Background of the Korean Conflict*   *31*

Three   •   *The Defense of the Pusan Beachhead*   *45*

Four   •   *"Handicaps? Inchon's Got 'Em All!"*   *62*

Five   •   *"Home for Christmas!"*   *78*

Six   •   *The Battle of Frozen Chosen*   *89*

Seven   •   *"Old Soldiers Never Die"*   *106*

Eight • Stalemate 119

Nine • Prisoners of the Communists 135

Medal of Honor Winners in the
Korean War 149

Books About the Korean War 153

Index 155

Korean
Chronology

1894-95

Sino-Japanese War. Korea is declared completely independent of China and Japan.

1904-05

Russo-Japanese War. After defeating Russia, Japan establishes a protectorate over Korea.

1910

Korea is annexed by Japan.

1943

At a meeting in Cairo, Egypt, during World War II President Franklin D. Roosevelt, Prime Minister Winston Churchill and Generalissimo Chiang Kai-shek promise independence to Korea.

1945

At a meeting of Allied leaders in Potsdam, Germany, Russian Premier Joseph Stalin agrees to Cairo declaration of eventual independence for Korea.

Following the defeat of Japan in World War II, Korea is divided at the 38th parallel into American and Russian occupation zones.

1948

United Nations commission appointed to organize democratic elections throughout Korea. Russia will not admit the commission into North Korea. Following the U.N.-sponsored elections, which are limited to South Korea, the Republic of Korea is established with Syngman Rhee as President.

Russia reports that its army of occupation has left North Korea.

1949

United States army of occupation withdraws from South Korea, leaving 500 American military advisers in the Republic.

Guerrilla activity takes place on both sides of the 38th parallel, and there are numerous border incidents involving troops of the rival Korean armies.

1950

June 25   North Korean Communist armies cross the 38th parallel in force, starting the war. United Nations issues a cease-fire order which is ignored by the Reds.

June 27-30   U.N. authorizes member nations to send military aid to South Korea. President Harry S. Truman orders U.S. ground forces into action.

July	7-8	General Douglas MacArthur is named commander of U.N. forces in Korea.
July-August		American and ROK troops retreat to Naktong River. U.S. and supporting forces battle to hold a beachhead (Pusan perimeter) in southeast corner of peninsula.
September	15	U.S. forces make an amphibious landing at Inchon.
September	26	U.S. forces recapture Seoul, capital of South Korea.
October	1-7	ROK and U.N. troops cross the 38th parallel and begin offensive in North Korea.
October	15	President Truman and General MacArthur meet on Wake Island.
October-November		U.N. forces capture Pyongyang, capital of North Korea, and drive toward Manchurian border. Chinese Communist troops enter the war.
November	26	Chinese Communists launch drive against the U.N. forces that eventually carries below the 38th parallel.
November	27	U.S. forces begin epic battle of "Frozen Chosen."
December	24	U.S. forces are successfully evacuated from Hungnam.

1951

January	4	Reds recapture Seoul a second time.
February	1	U.N. General Assembly brands People's Republic of China as an aggressor in Korea.
March-April		MacArthur warns of a stalemate unless his forces are allowed to attack Communist bases in Manchuria.
April	11	Truman relieves MacArthur as U.N. commander; replaces him with General

13

Matthew Ridgeway.

May-June		Reds launch all-out drive to destroy U.S. Eighth Army. U.S., ROK and supporting U.N. forces stop drive and launch counterattack.
June	*23*	Jacob Malik, Russia's representative to the U.N., says: "Discussions should start for a cease-fire."
July	*10*	Truce talks begin at Kaesong.
August	*23*	Reds suspend truce talks.
September	*13*	U.N. forces launch attacks to drive Reds back to the peace table.
October	*25*	Peace talks are resumed, moving to Panmunjom.

1952

January-June		Continued period of stalemate at the peace table and on the battlefield, United States casualties continue at a rate of 30,000 a year.
July-November		Peace talks enter their second year. Stalemate continues.
December	*2-5*	President-elect Dwight D. Eisenhower visits Korean battle areas.

1953

January	*25*	U.N. forces launch a general attack.
April	*20*	Operation "Little Switch," the exchange of sick and wounded prisoners, begins.
June	*17*	President Syngman Rhee orders the release of 27,000 anti-Communist North Korean prisoners of war.
July	*8*	Reds end truce talk stalemate.
July	*27*	Armistice is signed at Panmunjom after 37 months of fighting. Cease-fire begins at 10 P.M.
August-September		Operation "Big Switch," voluntary repatriation of prisoners, is completed.

Illustrations

MAP

The Korean Theater   *18*

PHOTOGRAPHS

Major General William F. Dean   *21*
The Security Council of the United Nations   *40*
General Douglas MacArthur   *43*
Lieutenant General Walton H. Walker   *47*
A Korean boy named Jimmy   *50*
Lieutenant William Hudson   *55*
Armorers load ammunition belt in wing of a fighter plane   *55*
U.S. Marines raise the American flag on Wolmi-do   *73*
Marines scale sea walls with hooked ladders to land at Inchon   *73*
U.S. Air Force F-86 Sabrejets patrol "MIG Alley" in Northwest
    Korea   *82*
Captain Joseph McConnell   *82*
Major James Jabara   *82*
Three U.S. riflemen try to dry themselves around a small fire during
    Korea's rainy season   *91*

15

Marines of the 5th and 7th Regiments withdraw from Yudam-ni on icy road   93

Marines retreat to Hagaru-ri, on the southern tip of the Chosen Reservoir   93

The Marines bring their equipment and their wounded with them on the retreat from Yudam-ni   97

Exhausted members of the 1st Marine Division on the road back from "Frozen Chosen"   97

Leathernecks catch a few minutes' rest during heroic breakout from Chosen Reservoir   102

Elements of 1st Marine Division rest on snow-covered roadside after overcoming an ambush   102

Riflemen take cover behind large boulders   104

A Marine Corsair gives close air support to fighters in Chosen Reservoir area   104

Lieutenant General Matthew B. Ridgeway   108

South of Koto-ri, the "attack in a different direction" nears Chinhung-ni and the sea   108

General MacArthur and Lieutenant General Matthew B. Ridgeway visit the front   113

The United Nations delegation, headed by Admiral C. Turner Joy, at Kaesong   121

The Communist delegation at first armistice meetings   121

U.S. infantrymen paid dearly to capture Bloody Ridge   124

A squad of American infantrymen man a ridge   129

An American G.I. and a ROK soldier at a defense position with automatic rifles   129

President-elect Dwight D. Eisenhower eats dinner with members of the 3rd Division during tour of Korean battlefront   132

Ike visits with other U.S. riflemen of the 3rd Division during battlefront tour   132

Lieutenant General Maxwell D. Taylor and General Mark Clark at the front with an officer of the Greek battalion   143

16

*The
United States
in
the Korean
War*

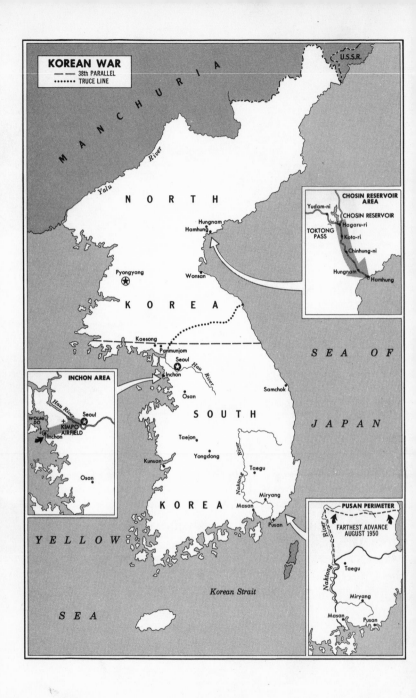

One

*The Capture
of
General Dean*

Sunday morning, June 25, 1950, was quiet and peaceful for the United States Army occupation forces in Kokura, Japan. It was, in fact, almost like a peacetime Sunday at home.

One of the officers attending church services this quiet Sunday morning was a friendly-faced, sandy-haired giant of a man standing over six feet tall and weighing more than two hundred pounds. On his collar were a major general's two stars and on one shoulder sleeve was the green taro leaf insignia of his division. This man was Major General William "Big Bill" Dean, commander of the United States 24th Infantry Division, combat veteran of World War II and former military governor of South Korea.

During the church services General Dean gave thanks for the fact that his assignment in Korea was ended and he would not be going back there again. Perhaps he and his wife, Mildred, who was with him here in Japan, would soon be returning to the States. It would be wonderful to see their daughter, June, and their son, Bill Jr., who was just about to enter West Point. As he strolled out of church, General Dean was feeling that God was indeed in his heaven and all was right with the world. At that moment the post duty officer came rushing up.

"General, sir, we've just had word that the North Koreans have crossed the 38th parallel and invaded South Korea."

"In force, or is it just another raid?" General Dean asked hopefully. There had been frequent border clashes between the North and South Koreans in recent months.

"In force, sir."

The general's face was suddenly worn and tired. Then the stern look of command glinted in his eyes and his voice was firm as he said, "Thank you. You'll have your orders shortly."

Later General Dean said to his wife, "Mildred, this is probably the start of the Third World War."

Mildred Dean did not falter even though she knew her husband would be in the thick of the fighting. "I'm grateful for one thing," she said.

"What's that?"

"June and Bill are safely out of it."

General Dean nodded. "Yes," he said with a wry smile, "and I thought we'd be seeing them soon."

But General Dean's main concern now was his division. He knew it was cut down to two-thirds of its wartime strength. And only a small percentage of his men were veterans of World War II. Their equipment was also out of date. Worst of all, the men were scattered all over Japan going through training exercises. It would

Major General William F. Dean   (U.S. Army Photograph)

take several days to get them together. General Dean knew he was faced with the most serious crisis in his career of more than a quarter of a century as a military man.

William Frishe Dean had wanted to be a soldier from the time he was a five-year-old boy. Born at Carlyle, Illinois, on August 1, 1899, he was the oldest of four children. In 1904 William's father, who was a dentist, took the boy to the St. Louis Exposition. There William watched some West Point cadets parade and his interest in becoming a soldier began. As soon as he returned to Carlyle, he started doing daily body-building exercises, a habit he continued into manhood. As a man he would also walk at least five miles a day and never ride an elevator if he could run up a flight of stairs.

William was an outstanding student, graduating as valedictorian of his Carlyle high school class in 1918. Immediately after graduation, he tried unsuccessfully to get into West Point. He also tried to join the Army so he could go overseas with General Pershing's American Expeditionary Forces in World War I, but he was under age and his mother refused to give him permission to enlist.

Shortly after the war the Dean family moved to California, and William enrolled at the University of California. He took a prelaw course but was not nearly so interested in his studies as he was in the Students' Army Training Corps, which he joined as a freshman. He worked his way through college at a variety of jobs — dock worker, street car conductor and motorman, dishwasher and even as a part-time policeman on the Berkeley police force.

After he got out of college William served briefly with the National Guard and was finally commissioned a second lieutenant in the regular Army on October 18, 1923. His first assignment was with the infantry at Fort

Douglas, Utah. Then began a long, hard period of apprenticeship. He was to remain a lieutenant for 12 years, but they would be important years in which he learned his soldier's trade.

While at Fort Douglas, Lieutenant Dean met and fell in love with Mildred Dern whose home was in Salt Lake City. The young lieutenant's only possessions at this time were several horses which he prized. He sold them to pay for his wedding to Mildred on August 25, 1926.

During the 1920's and 1930's Dean served at a number of Army posts and attended several Army schools, including the Command and General Staff School at Fort Leavenworth, Kansas. At the start of World War II he was a major, and by 1942 he had been made a colonel. He was serving at a desk job in Washington, however, and he requested that he be assigned to combat duty. Finally he was made a brigadier general and named assistant commander of the 44th Infantry Division which sailed for France in August 1944.

In December 1944 Dean became the division's commander, leading his men in hard-fought action against the Nazis through Germany and Austria. The 44th captured some 30,000 German prisoners and helped force the surrender of the 19th German Army. Dean was awarded the Bronze Star, the Distinguished Service Medal, and for "extraordinary heroism" in combat the Distinguished Service Cross.

After World War II Major General Dean was named military governor of South Korea and deputy commander of the American occupation forces there. While he was military governor, South Korea held its first free elections in 4,000 years. After Syngman Rhee was inaugurated as the first president of the Republic of Korea, Dean served for a time as Chief of Staff of the United States 8th Army under Lieutenant General Walton Walker. As had always been the case in the past, however, Dean wanted to serve with infantry troops. He got his wish when Walker appointed him commander of the 24th Infantry — the division General Dean was now assembling for combat duty in South Korea, just 140 miles away. He had always been a frontline commander. Once again he would personally lead his men into action.

Seven North Korean infantry divisions and one armored division had driven south across the 38th parallel in the early dawn hours of June 25 (Korean time). Their main blow was aimed at Seoul, the Republic of Korea's capital city. The invaders numbered about 100,-000 men, with many more thousands in reserve. Most of them were battle-seasoned veterans who had fought with the Chinese Communists or Russians in World War II. They were well-trained and well-equipped with Russian tanks and aircraft.

Defending against these invading forces along the 38th parallel were four Republic of Korea (ROK) divisions made up of about 40,000 men. There were four more partially trained ROK divisions further behind the lines, including one at Seoul. Most of the front-line ROK soldiers had been trained by the United States, but they had no tanks, no heavy artillery, no anti-tank weapons and no combat aircraft. The ROK defensive forces were, in short, no match at all for the tough, hard-hitting North Korean enemy.

Seoul fell on June 28. By the first week in July the North Koreans had penetrated in several places to points some 50 miles below the 38th parallel and were threatening to overrun the entire peninsula. The retreating ROK forces became so disorganized that there was a very real danger that they might suffer total defeat before aid could arrive from Japan. It was General Dean's job to get his men to South Korea and perform the most difficult of all military feats: fight a delaying action against overwhelming odds.

The first United States fighting unit to be sent to South Korea by General Dean was called Task Force Smith. This was a group of some 400 infantrymen and an artillery battery led by Lieutenant Colonel Charles B. (Brad) Smith.

Colonel Smith was in bed asleep on the night of June 30, 1950, when General Dean's orders arrived alerting him for Korean duty. By a curious coincidence Brad Smith had also been rudely awakened to take command of an infantry unit on Sunday morning, December 7, 1941, at Oahu, Hawaii, when the Japanese bombed Pearl Harbor.

General Dean told Colonel Smith that his task force was to be flown to Pusan, a city at the southern tip of the Korean peninsula. From there it was to travel by truck convoy to Taejon in the middle of South Korea. With Seoul now in enemy hands, Taejon had become the provisional capital of the Republic of Korea.

"I'll meet you there," General Dean said. "Good luck, and God bless you." The two men shook hands solemnly.

Within the next few days General Dean got the rest of the 24th Division under way for Korea — a part of it was airborne and a part of it traveled by troop ship and truck — and then on July 3 he flew to Taejon to join some of his men who had already arrived there. He encountered a scene of almost complete confusion. ROK troops were in full retreat along the roads and railroads leading south. To make matters worse, countless Korean civilian refugees also jammed the roads as they fled desperately before the onrushing enemy.

25

Dean tried to rally the ROK troops, but they told him they couldn't stop tanks simply by hurling men at them. They continued to retreat. On July 4 General Dean ordered Task Force Smith into action at Osan, a city on the main road north of Taejon and 30 miles south of Seoul. If this road could be blocked until more troops arrived from Japan, Taejon might yet be saved.

Task Force Smith was attacked on July 5 by an entire North Korean division supported by more than 30 tanks. In this flaming battle the first United States Army artillery shell of the Korean War was fired and the first American soldiers were killed. Smith's unit suffered severe losses in men and equipment and the delaying action failed.

It now became clear to General Dean that Taejon would fall, but he did not intend to give up without a fight. Every hour that he could delay the enemy's advance would mean that much more time to get American infantry troops into South Korea. He had considered making Taejon the expeditionary force headquarters. With the defeat of Task Force Smith, Dean transferred his command post to Yongdong a dozen miles further south, but he remained in Taejon.

Early on the morning of July 20 Dean got word that enemy tanks had entered the outskirts of the city. He decided to go tank hunting. The outnumbered infantrymen of the 24th Division who were defending Taejon had already done a good job of destroying enemy armor and at first all Dean could find were dead tanks. Shortly, however, he encountered two live ones. By this time the general had found a G.I. with a bazooka, but the G.I. had only a single round for his weapon. The G.I. managed to get in a shot but missed the target. Angry and desperate, General Dean threw the only grenade he had at the tank. Then, despite the machine-gun bullets that sprayed from its turrets, Dean stood in the middle of the street and fired his .45 pistol at the metal monster.

Dean finally found some more rounds for the bazooka, and he and the G.I. took up a defensive position in the upper story of a building. From here they managed to destroy at least one tank in the face of severe cannon and machine-gun fire. Some of Dean's men were now attacking the enemy armor with recently arrived American tanks, and Dean recklessly exposed himself to point out targets for his gunners. His efforts were successful when several more North Korean tanks were destroyed by cannon fire. By nightfall, however, the general decided it was time to get out of the city.

Dean and his aides organized two convoys of vehicles to start for division headquarters at Yongdong. The general and his aides in two jeeps were in the second and last convoy to leave the dying city. They had not driven far before they ran into the tail of the first column, which had been ambushed. Sniper and machine-gun fire flamed all around the general's jeep as he and his aides raced down the road. In their haste to get through the roadblock they missed the intersection of the road to Yongdong. Dean felt certain, however, that they could get to their destination by making a detour.

A few miles further along the road they ran into more ambushed American vehicles. Dean ordered his driver to stop to pick up the wounded. Again they got under way, but they had driven only a short distance before enemy fire drove them off the road. Immediately Dean and his men began to crawl away through the bushes to avoid capture.

The situation was a desperate one, but Dean believed they could make their way safely to friendly territory. During the night he helped carry one of the severely wounded men who seemed to be dying of thirst. The wounded man emptied every available canteen and continued to cry out for water. When the group of escaping men finally stopped for a brief rest, General Dean thought he heard the sound of water trickling nearby. He decided to go in search of it. The night was pitch black and he had walked only a few steps when he suddenly stumbled down a steep hill, lost his balance, fell and knocked himself out.

When he came to, the general had no idea how long he had been lying unconscious. It was still dark, but he realized the others must have gone on without him. He also realized he had severely gashed his head and injured his shoulder. He would not regain full use of his shoulder for almost a year.

A short time later Dean managed to find some water, but again he passed out. When he came to, it was nearing dawn. He heard an enemy patrol nearby and now he felt certain that if the other men of his command had not gone on without him, they had been captured. He crawled into a thick clump of bushes and hid there for the rest of the day. That night he started walking toward what he believed were the American lines.

There now began for General Dean an incredible 35 days in which he wandered through the hills of South Korea. Severely injured, almost without food, uncertain of his directions, not knowing whether villages contained friends or enemies, wondering if the war might already have been lost, the gallant general nevertheless was fiercely determined that he would never be captured. He had a revolver, and he polished its parts daily to make certain it was in working order, so if he were threatened with capture he could go down fighting.

For 20 days General Dean went completely without

food. During this time he figured he lost almost 75 pounds. Occasionally he managed to find some dried up fruit in orchards or was given a meager meal of millet or rice and pork fat by South Koreans. For the most part, however, the Koreans tried to ignore him. Sometimes children saw him and reported his presence to their parents. They in turn reported him to the local police, who tried to capture him. When he did get food he ate ravenously, remembering — particularly as he wolfed down the pork fat — that when he was a boy back in Carlyle, his parents had always told him he left too much fat on his plate.

At the end of a month, when Dean was very near death from starvation and exposure, he met two South Koreans who appeared friendly. They were Han Doo Kyoo, 40, and Choi Chong Bong, 24. They told Dean they would lead him to safety. The general was suspicious but accepted their offer. Within a short time Dean's two "friends" turned him over to the North Korean Communists. Their reward, it was later learned, amounted to the equivalent of $5.00.

When General Dean realized he had been betrayed, he tried to draw his revolver but one of his "friends" grabbed his right arm in a bulldog grip. Nevertheless, Dean continued to struggle shouting at his captors, "Go ahead, shoot me! Shoot me! Get it over with!" He actually hoped they would shoot him because he knew what tremendous propaganda value there was for the North Korean Communists in having captured not only an American general officer but also the former military governor of South Korea. His captors managed to subdue him, however.

General Dean was taken prisoner on August 25, which was his and Mildred Dean's 24th wedding anniversary. Back in Japan, Mildred Dean had no idea what had happened to her husband, nor had anybody in the Army high command any information to give her. The last reports out of Taejon told of the general fighting tanks in the streets. Later his bullet-scarred helmet was found near the city, leading everyone to suspect that Dean had been killed. It would be almost a year and a half before Mildred Dean and the anxious people of America would learn the heroic general's fate.

Meanwhile, unknown to General Dean in his solitary cell in North Korea, he would be the first person in the Korean War to win the nation's highest award for valor. On September 30, 1950, General Dean was awarded the Congressional Medal of Honor *in absentia*. The citation accompanying his award for heroism read: "He personally and alone attacked an enemy tank while armed only with a hand grenade. He also directed the fire of his own tanks from an exposed position with neither cover nor concealment while under observed artillery and small arms fire. When the town of Taejon was finally overrun he refused to insure his own safety by leaving with the leading elements but remained behind organizing his retreating forces, directing stragglers, and was last seen assisting the wounded to a place of safety."

Two

*Background
of the
Korean
Conflict*

Long before 1950 Korea had become familiar with the tragedy of war. Only slightly larger than the state of Kansas, Korea was nevertheless prized by China and Russia as an overland route to the Pacific and by Japan as a gateway to Asia. Korea's powerful neighbors used the narrow peninsula, about 150 miles wide and some 600 miles long, for invasions and counterinvasions that laid waste to the land. Few countries have seen so much bloodshed.

In its early history Korea, or Chosen ("land of the morning calm") as it was then called, was strongly influenced by China. Under the Chinese it reached a high level of power, wealth and culture. In 1403, for example, almost half a century before Johann Gutenberg, the Koreans used movable type for printing.

Late in the 16th century Japan invaded Korea and occupied the country for several years. The Japanese were finally driven out after the Koreans scored a naval victory over Japan by using ironclad ships shaped like turtles. The Koreans then tried for more than two centuries to keep their borders closed to all foreigners. Although they were not wholly successful in this effort, their land did become known as the Hermit Kingdom.

Western nations had now become interested in Korea, but the main rivals for its control were China and Japan. In 1894 this rivalry resulted in the Sino-Japanese War. Chinese troops were easily driven from the peninsula by the Japanese in 1895. After this, both China and Japan said they would recognize Korea's independence. Japan did not keep this bargain. It continued to interfere in Korea's government.

By now Russia had begun to extend its power into Manchuria and other areas of the Far East. To prevent Japan from having a free hand in Korea, Russia offered military instructors to train the Korean army. Continued disagreements between Russia and Japan finally led to the Russo-Japanese War of 1904-05 from which Japan emerged as the victor and a world power. To end the war a peace conference was arranged at Portsmouth, New Hampshire, by United States President Theodore Roosevelt. In the Treaty of Portsmouth, Japan's rights in Korea were recognized not only by Russia but also by Great Britain who had backed Japan in the war, and the United States

From 1905 to World War II Japanese control of Korea was complete. The nation was turned into a "rice bowl" to increase the food supply of the Japanese home islands Its mines and industries enriched Japan. Koreans were not allowed to speak their native language, and worship of the Japanese emperor was taught in their schools. Any and all signs of independence were ruthlessly suppressed by the police and the Japanese army. By World War II there was one policeman for every 400 Koreans.

Nevertheless, the Koreans resisted, and thousands were killed or imprisoned. Even this treatment did not put an end to their patriotic uprisings. Groups of nationalists continued to meet in Korea as well as outside the country and issue proclamations of independence. One of the leaders in this fight for freedom was a young man by the name of Lee Sung Man, or Syngman Rhee as he chose to call himself after he attended a Methodist missionary school in Korea where he learned English and became a Christian.

Syngman Rhee has often been called the "George Washington of Korea." Born on April 26, 1875, he became a leader in patriotic groups while he was still a young student. He also founded and edited the first Korean daily newspaper, *Independence,* which was fearlessly outspoken in its criticism of the Japanese. In 1904 he was forced to flee the country, and he came to the United States.

Soon after his arrival he began trying to get Americans to help save his country from Japan. Before the Portsmouth peace meeting at the end of the Russo-Japanese War, Rhee went directly to President Roosevelt and requested that Korea have a seat at the conference. His request was denied, as were his pleas that the United States refuse to recognize Japanese "rights" in Korea.

Rhee attended school in the United States. He received his B.A. degree from George Washington University in 1907, his M.A. from Harvard in 1908, and his Ph.D. in international law from Princeton in 1910. Woodrow Wilson, who was then president of Princeton, personally handed Rhee his doctoral degree, the first to be awarded a Korean by an American university.

In 1911 Rhee returned to Korea, where he spent a year and a half doing Y.M.C.A. work and teaching. Once again, however, he was forced to flee when he learned that the Japanese were planning to put him in jail.

Rhee remained a dedicated patriot. At home and abroad he continued to fight for Korean independence. In 1919 a group of Korean nationalists meeting secretly at Seoul elected him the head of the nation's government in exile, a post he held for the next 20 years. He continued to earn his living by teaching.

In 1939 Rhee went to Washington, where he spent much of his time trying to gain U.S. recognition of Korea. His struggle to free his country finally began to bear fruit during World War II.

At a meeting of Allied leaders at Cairo, Egypt, in December 1943 China, Great Britain and the United States promised that Korea would be given its independence "in due course" after World War II. At an Allied conference at Potsdam, Germany, in July 1945 this promise was repeated and Russia agreed to it.

On August 6, 1945, the United States dropped an atomic bomb on Hiroshima, Japan. Two days later Russia, realizing that the conflict was all but ended and wanting to get a share of the Far East spoils, declared war on Japan. On August 9, a second atom bomb was dropped, this time on Nagasaki, and on August 10 the Japanese asked for peace terms. A few days later Japan laid down its arms, but Russian troops were already in Korea. United States troops did not arrive in Korea until almost a month later.

Meanwhile, it had been agreed — almost casually — that the United States would accept the surrender of all Japanese troops in Korea below the 38th parallel and Russia would accept the surrender of all Japanese troops above that line. The division of Korea at the 38th parallel was never intended to be permanent, but the Russians immediately began to organize North Korea as a separate Communist state.

At Moscow in December 1945 Russia agreed that Korea should be allowed to set up its own provisional government. The United States tried for more than a year and a half to get Russia to live up to this agreement, but without success. Finally, in September 1947, the United States asked that the thorny problem of establishing Korean independence be placed before the United Nations, the international peace organization that had been born out of the high hopes for world freedom during World War II. Its success or failure in solving the Korean problem could mean the success or failure of the United Nations as an effective organization.

At the end of World War I an organization similar to the United Nations had been founded. This was the League of Nations. It failed in its purpose partly because the United States refused to become a member, despite President Woodrow Wilson's dedicated efforts. It also failed, however, because the nations that were members of the League did not live up to their pledges to take the necessary steps to halt the armed attacks of one country upon another. Now the United Nations was faced with the same decision.

The United Nations had its beginnings in 1941 when President Franklin D. Roosevelt and Prime Minister Winston Churchill issued the Atlantic Charter, which promised that the use of force among nations would be abandoned and some sort of "permanent system of general security" would be set up. The following year 26 countries sent representatives to a meeting in Washington, D. C. They agreed to the principles of the Atlantic

Charter. In 1944 actual plans were drawn up for the organization of the United Nations.

In the spring of 1945 a United Nations conference attended by delegates from 50 nations met at San Francisco. The organization's charter was completed in June. This time the United States was determined to become a member of the organization for world peace. The U.S. Senate ratified the U.N. charter on July 28, 1945. The required number of other nations also ratified the charter, and on October 24, 1945, the U.N. officially came into existence.

When the U.N. was presented with the problem of establishing Korean independence, it passed a resolution stating that free elections should be held there in 1948. Russia refused to allow such an election in North Korea. Despite Soviet claims that it was illegal, the election was held in South Korea on May 10, 1948. On August 15 Syngman Rhee became president of the Republic of Korea with its capital at Seoul. (In the Korean language, Seoul means capital.)

In North Korea the Communists inaugurated a so-called People's Democratic Republic on September 9, with its capital at Pyongyang. This was a typical Russian "tank-and-infantry democracy," with military and police authority dictating the "free" activities of the people. With the establishment of separate governments in North and South Korea, the 38th parallel became an armed frontier separating two enemy forces.

Between the end of World War II and the inauguration of the Republic of Korea, the U.S. kept military occupation troops in South Korea, and the Russians occupied North Korea in force. It was during this period that General Dean had been the military governor of South Korea. Under General Dean, U.S. troops trained the

South Korean army. After the inauguration of the Republic of Korea, American occupation forces were withdrawn. By the spring of 1949 all that remained were some 500 U.S. military advisers.

The Russians also announced that they had withdrawn their troops, but the Soviets would not allow U.N. inspection of the area. The North Korean Communists also did their best to strangle South Korea's economy by sabotage and other means and conducted frequent border raids and guerrilla actions below the 38th parallel. In addition, Russia itself did everything possible to disrupt the government of the Republic of Korea. It did so through false propaganda issued at the U.N. and elsewhere throughout the world about Syngman Rhee and his aides. The peace between the North and South Koreans had been an uneasy one right up to the morning of June 25, 1950, when the North Korean Communists decided to conquer South Korea by military force.

Trygve Lie was the first Secretary General of the United Nations. When word of the invasion of South Korea reached the Western world, Lie exclaimed angrily, "This is war against the United Nations!"

A Norwegian, Lie had seen his country ruled by force under the Nazis in World War II. He was determined that no other small and helpless nation should suffer a similar fate in the future. Lie called an emergency meeting of the Security Council, the U.N. organization with the power to take strong enforcement measures to preserve peace.

During this period Russia was boycotting meetings of the Security Council because the U.N. had refused to accept Red China as a member. Russia's failure to have a representative at the Security Council meetings during the early part of the Korean crisis made it possible for the

Council to act swiftly and decisively against the North Korean invaders. Had a Russian representative been present, he probably would have uttered the traditional Russian negative, "Nyet," thus vetoing any positive action. As it was, when Russia did return to the meetings it insisted all action taken during its absence was illegal.

The emergency meeting was held on Sunday, June 25, New York time. (Because of the International Date Line, Korean time is 14 hours earlier than Eastern Standard Time.) At this meeting a resolution was passed calling for the "immediate cessation of hostilities." It also called upon the North Koreans "to withdraw forthwith their armed forces to the 38th parallel."

Meanwhile, U.S. President Harry S. Truman was in Independence, Missouri, for the weekend when news of the crisis reached Washington. He returned to the capital immediately and met with his military leaders to decide on a course of action. These leaders knew that, just as in World War I and World War II, the United States was caught unprepared to fight a war. This time, however, the United States had no Allies to hold off the enemy while it armed. The main responsibility for the defense of Korea would immediately fall on the United States.

It soon became clear that the North Korean Communists had no intention of halting their invasion troops. Their intention was to overrun the entire Korean peninsula as quickly as possible, before any serious military defense could be mounted against them. This too was a typical Russian tactic: to present the world with an accomplished conquest and then debate about it. Once the peninsula was in their hands they knew debate and resolutions on the part of the U.N. would be useless. A vacuum had been created in Korea, and in true Communist fashion the North Koreans were filling it by conquest before the free world could decide what to do about it.

This time, however, the free world did know what to do about it. The United Nations, and particularly the United States, moved and moved more swiftly and effectively than the Communists believed possible.

The U.N. Security Council now passed a second resolution. This resolution recommended that "the members of the United Nations furnish such assistance to the Republic of Korea as may be necessary to repel the armed attack and restore the international peace and security in the area." Thus the U.N. succeeded in meeting its first challenge where the old League of Nations had failed.

On June 27 President Truman ordered the United States Air Force and Navy to support South Korea. The next day he authorized the use of United States Army infantry units in Korea. This was the order that sent General Dean's 24th Division to the beleaguered peninsula. Additional orders from the President authorized General Douglas MacArthur, who was the United States Commander in Chief in the Far East, to use all air, ground and naval forces to repel the invasion and set up a blockade of the entire Korean coast.

Early in July the Security Council recommended that a unified command be set up in Korea. It also requested that the United States name the unified commander. President Truman named General MacArthur to this post on July 8. Less than a week later President Syngman Rhee placed all ROK military forces under MacArthur. For the first time in its brief history, the fledgling United Nations was sending a fighting force into the field.

Of the 53 nations that signed the U.N. resolution to repel the enemy invaders, 16 eventually sent combat forces to aid the Republic of Korea. These nations were Australia, Belgium, Canada, Colombia, Ethiopia, France,

The Security Council of the United Nations on July 7, 1950, adopted a resolution recommending a unified command under the United States for the forces fighting in Korea. There were seven votes in favor of the resolution, none against it. (U.N. Photo)

Great Britain, Greece, Luxemburg, the Netherlands, New Zealand, the Philippines, Thailand, Turkey, the Union of South Africa and the United States. Five nations sent medical units. These were Denmark, India, Italy, Norway and Sweden.

Most of these nations sent a relatively small number of fighting men. Only the United States, Great Britain and Turkey sent more than an infantry battalion. Among the U.N. Allies, the United States bore the brunt of the fighting during the 37 months of the war with a force of some 300,000 Army ground troops, plus about 50,000 combat members of the Air Force, Navy and Marines. At their peak the U.N. forces in support of the U.S. reached a total of 33,000 infantrymen and 1,000 flyers and sailors. The First British Commonwealth Division made up of troops from Australia, Canada, Great Britain and New Zealand was the only non-Korean or non-American division in the field. The Republic of Korea, which was not a member of the U.N., eventually had 16 infantry divisions in the field, numbering some 400,000 men, or more than all of the United Nations forces combined.

Casualty figures give an even clearer picture of the relative number of men who saw action from the various U.N. countries and the Republic of Korea. The ROK army suffered an estimated 850,000 combat casualties, including more than 400,000 dead and more than 400,000 wounded or missing in action. Throughout the war the ROK army had to be brought up to strength with a steady flow of replacements. Some of its units suffered a 100 per cent casualty rate. In addition, in South Korea more than two and one-half million persons lost their homes and about one million civilians were killed.

The United States had more than 136,000 casualties, including about 34,000 killed and more than 103,000 wounded. None of the other U.N. nations suffered as many as 1,000 men killed in action, although both Great Britain and Turkey had more than 3,000 total casualties, including killed and wounded.

In the final analysis, however, it was not the number of men sent by each country that was important. What was truly important was the fact that this was the first United Nations war, the first time in history that the nations of the free world had banded together under the blue and white U.N. flag to halt aggression.

Many problems were involved in handling this mixed command. There were difficulties over differences in languages, diet, habits and customs — all of which taxed the skill of American commanders. In one instance, for example, United States General Sam Williams found that Turkish troops serving with American G.I.'s refused to take showers. A man dedicated to cleanliness, General Williams insisted that the Turks bathe. Finally the Turks obeyed his orders — but they took showers in their underwear. It took General Williams some time to discover that it was not the Turkish custom to disrobe in public. The problem was solved by building separate, enclosed showers.

There was also plenty of healthy competition among the U.N. troops. The Belgian battalion, for example, was attached to the U.S. 15th Infantry Regiment which proudly called itself the "Can Do" outfit. One day a Belgian jeep appeared with the slogan boldly painted on its side: "Belgians Can Do Too!"

It was with such spirit that the United Nations Command under General MacArthur went to work to retrieve victory from the jaws of defeat after the North Korean Communists moved across the 38th parallel with guns blazing on June 25, 1950. The North Koreans soon

General Douglas MacArthur, Commander in Chief, U.N. Command, is shown during press conference in Korea. (U.S. Army Photograph)

captured Seoul and Taejon and began to drive toward Taegu and Pusan at the tip of the South Korean peninsula. It was here in the Pusan beachhead, after General Dean's capture at Taejon, that the United States finally was able to bring enough defensive military weight to bear to stave off total defeat and prepare for an offensive that would drive the enemy back across the 38th parallel.

Three

*The Defense
of
the Pusan
Beachhead*

The summer of 1950 was a time of bitter defeat for the United States forces in Korea. The 25th Infantry and 1st Cavalry Divisions had followed General Dean's 24th Division from Japan to South Korea, and they too had been smashed into reeling retreat by the enemy. By late July these three American army divisions and the remnants of the ROK army had been driven into the southeast corner of the peninsula around the key port of Pusan.

This defense area was not much more than a beachhead. It was rectangular in shape and was guarded by two natural barriers — the Naktong River on the west and high mountains on the north. The outer rim or *perimeter* of the defense line measured about 150 miles in length. A final stand had to be made here if the defenders did not want to be driven into the sea.

In mid-July General MacArthur had announced that Lieutenant General Walton Walker, commander of the United States 8th Army in Japan, would be in charge of all United Nations and ROK ground troops in Korea. General Walker minced no words regarding the defense of the Pusan beachhead, or Pusan perimeter as it was more often called. He told his troops:

"There will be no more retreating, withdrawal, readjustment of the lines, or whatever else you want to call it. There are no lines behind us to which we can retreat. This is not going to be a Dunkirk or Bataan. A retreat to Pusan would result in one of the greatest butcheries in history. We must fight until the end. We will fight as a team. If some of us must die, we will die fighting together."

General Walker's "stand-or-die" order was headlined by newspapers in the United States. His words had a defiant ring to them that reminded many readers of America's great combat leader of World War II, General George "Blood-and-Guts" Patton. The public was not surprised to learn that Walker had served under Patton in Europe, where he had led a series of slashing armored attacks against the Nazis.

In his first assignment in Korea, however, Walker had to fight a different kind of battle. With his forces on the defensive he had to put out the fires of enemy attacks all along the Pusan perimeter, making sure that no major breakthrough-fire took place. By shuttling his fire-brigade forces from one threatened area to another it was up to Walker to save the United Nations from total defeat.

Lieutenant General Walton "Johnny" Walker was born on December 3, 1889, at Belton, Texas. His father was a storekeeper, and both of his grandfathers had been officers in the Confederate army during the Civil War.

Lieutenant General Walton H. Walker (U.S. Army Photograph)

The boy never wanted to be anything but a soldier.

After attending the military academy in Belton he enrolled at Virginia Military Institute, where he remained for a year before entering West Point in 1908. He was graduated from the United States Military Academy in 1912 and was then assigned to the infantry at Fort Sheridan, Illinois.

Young Walker served at various Army posts in the United States before World War I. In the spring of 1918 he went to France with the A.E.F. as a major in command of a machine-gun battalion and saw action at St. Mihiel and in the Meuse-Argonne campaign. For gallantry under fire he was awarded the Silver Star and after the Armistice was promoted to lieutenant colonel.

Colonel Walker returned to the United States after serving with the army of occupation in Germany until 1919. In 1924 he married Caroline Emerson of Baltimore. They had one son, Sam Sims Walker, who later attended West Point and was an officer in the 82nd Airborne Division at the time of the Korean War.

Between World War I and World War II Walker's aggressive spirit finally resulted in his being assigned to duty with the newly organized armored forces. When the United States entered World War II, Walker became a major general in charge of the armored forces desert training center in California. Here the stocky, heavy-set General Walker said bluntly:

"I believe in making training so tough that combat will seem easy."

A month and a half after the Allies invaded Normandy in 1944, General Patton's 3rd Army started its famous victory drive across France and Germany and into Austria. General Walker's 20th Corps spearheaded this drive. Walker's efforts were praised not only by Patton but also by General Dwight Eisenhower, the U.S. War Department and Prime Minister Winston Churchill, who spoke about his feats in the House of Commons. Walker was awarded the Distinguished Service Cross and an Oak Leaf Cluster to his Silver Star and promoted to lieutenant general.

After the war Walker was placed in command of the United States 8th Army in occupied Japan. He was immediately aware of the fact that his rookie troops were soft from their easy life of occupation duty. Most of them were also without combat experience. He started a tough combat-training course in an effort to ready his men for possible action. Through no fault of his own General Walker was not wholly successful in this effort. Neither his troops nor the American people seemed interested in what General Walker called "the grave responsibility of preparedness."

As soon as World War II ended, there had been a great demand from American mothers and fathers to send their boys home from overseas. The servicemen joined in the clamor to be discharged, and soon the greatest military force the world had ever seen was all but destroyed.

Once again, as they always had in the past, the professional career men in the Army, Navy and Air Force had tried to bring some order out of the chaos caused by reducing the size of their commands and the amount of money available for preparedness. But right up to the start of the Korean War they had been fighting something of a losing battle. The public had even demanded that service discipline be less severe, and military leaders found themselves unable to get their men ready for combat when orders were often obeyed by civilian draftees only if they felt like obeying them.

Many of the green troops that General Walker had

A Korean boy named Jimmy was temporarily adopted by United States sailors during the fighting near Pusan. Other Korean boys of about Jimmy's age later helped the Navy perform an important intelligence mission before the amphibious landings at Inchon. (Official U.S. Navy Photograph)

tried to train for combat had now seen their first grim action in the so-called Korean "conflict." They had arrived expecting to spend only a short time taking part in a "police action," which was how President Truman had described their role. This led to many wry comments on the part of the men who were sent to Korea.

"If I'm a policeman, where's my badge?" some of them asked.

And when they began to be wounded and killed in the brutal fighting against the North Korean Communists, they were soon aware that this was indeed war, no matter what name the people at home gave it.

As a result of the softness of occupation life in Japan, some Americans fled in retreat on their first contact with the enemy. In these "bug-outs" the men sometimes threw away their weapons without firing a shot. It was this "bug-out" atmosphere that caused General Walker to make his "stand-or-die" order.

Tragically, General Walker himself had only a few short months to live. He would be killed in a jeep accident on December 23, 1950. By a strange coincidence Walker's World War II commander, General Patton, had also died as the result of injuries suffered in an automobile accident, in Germany just five years earlier. Before his death, however, Walker succeeded in rallying his men in a gallant stand along the fire-swept front of the Pusan perimeter. In doing so, he proved himself to be one of the great generals of the Korean War.

There was hard and bitter fighting all along the Pusan perimeter during August and early September 1950. Much of the fighting resulted from the North Koreans' attempts to cross the Naktong River and breach General Walker's defense lines. Occasionally the enemy made a minor breakthrough, and then savage fighting took place to recapture the lost ground. Walker and his warriors managed to hang on, but they hung on by their finger-nails.

Meanwhile, a reserve of men and equipment — including all-important tanks — was being built up in the beach-head. This reserve poured into the port of Pusan and was quickly moved to the front.

The fighting at the front was like nothing the United States Army men — even those who were combat veterans of World War II — had ever seen before. First of all, there was the heat. One-hundred-degree temperatures were common, and the constant rain added to the discomfort. Then there were the never-ending Korean hills that had to be captured and recaptured in the seesaw battles along the banks of the Naktong. As many casualties were caused by the heat and exhaustion from battling up these hills carrying and hauling equipment as were caused by the enemy. Salt tablets became as important as weapons and ammunition. Many men also suffered from severe stomach trouble from eating locally grown vetetables which the South Koreans fertilized with human waste. Finally there was the enemy himself — a hard, well-trained, tire-less foe who could fight seemingly without let-up and live on two or three rice balls a day.

The average North Korean combat division carried with it only about 70 tons of supplies. By comparison, seven tons of shipping were required to put each Ameri-can infantryman ashore, plus a ton of supplies a month to keep him in combat. But the North Korean army was severely handicapped by its slim diet. When its men cap-tured a town they stopped fighting to gorge themselves on food, and thus they often failed to take full advantage of their immediate military successes. The Red leaders never seemed to punish their men for such actions, however. In fact they themselves often took part in the looting and pillaging of villages. The North Koreans also seemed to pay no attention to the number of their own casualties, which were often enormous.

The North Korean "Human Sea" attacks were also new to the G.I.'s — new and frightening. Several waves of men were used. The first waves were sent forward in great numbers to overwhelm the defenders. When these waves were mowed down, others followed, in an attempt to make the defenders use up all of their ammunition. Then followed a final wave of veteran troops that often succeeded in capturing the position.

General Walker's headquarters were at Taegu, which was situated near the middle of the beachhead. From here Walker directed his fire-brigade ground forces and also worked closely with Major General Earl E. Partridge, commander of the United States 5th Air Force which was part of the Far East Air Forces.

Air and ground forces cooperated brilliantly to stop the enemy. If there was a sudden North Korean attack against a weak defensive position, General Partridge ordered his planes to fill the breach. If there was a temporary breakthrough, Walker requested air support from Partridge to bomb and machine-gun the advancing enemy until infantry reserves could be hurried into action. Since Walker was often down to as little as a company of men in reserve, quick air action frequently meant the difference between successful defense and sudden disaster.

The 5th Air Force had roared into combat on the second day of the war. Its transport planes — C-46's, C-47's and C-54's — had been flown to Seoul to evacuate American civilians from the doomed South Korean capital. They were protected on these missions by F-51 Mustang fighters and F-82 Twin Mustangs.

On June 27 Lieutenant Colonel James W. Little and First Lieutenant William G. Hudson were flying protective cover for several unarmed C-54's when a pair of Russian-built North Korean YAK fighter planes tried to attack the transports. Little and Hudson met the attack head on, and their blazing guns sent the YAK's down in flames. Lieutenant Hudson was credited with the first official aerial "kill" of the war.

American flyers quickly took complete control of the air over Korea. Most of the aircraft and the men who flew them were battle-tested veterans of World War II. In addition to the transports left over from World War II, there were a number of old but useful B-26 medium bombers and B-29 Superfortresses based in Japan. The fighter planes used early in the Korean conflict also dated back to the last war. Later, the new jets — the F-80 Shooting Star, the F-84 Thunderjet, and the F-86 Sabrejet, which gained fame as the "MIG Killer" — made headline news, but in the early days of the fighting it was the old warhorses of the runways that once again roared into action to rule the skies. Outstanding among these planes was the F-51 Mustang.

The F-51 had been called the P-51 in World War II, and late in that conflict it proved to be one of the finest fighter planes ever built. But the early history of the "Pea Shooter," as the P-51 was affectionately nicknamed, had been curiously unsuccessful.

Originally it was manufactured for the British Royal Air Force by an American aircraft firm. In 1941 and 1942 the RAF used the P-51 to fly in close support of attacking infantry troops, but it was a failure in this role. In 1943 the United States Air Forces used the "Pea Shooter" as a dive-bomber in the Mediterranean theater of war. This effort was also unsuccessful, and gradually the plane fell into disfavor.

Lieutenant William Hudson, who was credited with the first aerial "kill" of the Korean War. (U.S. Air Force Photo)

Armorers are shown loading .50 caliber ammunition belts in the wing of an F-51 Mustang fighter plane. (U.S. Army Photograph)

In the summer of 1943, however, when the United States 8th Air Force was searching desperately for a long-range fighter plane to accompany its heavy bombers all the way to their European targets and back, the P-51 Mustang was suddenly rediscovered. The RAF had placed Rolls Royce Merlin engines in their P-51's and the results were sensational. The plane with its new Merlin engine proved every bit as good as the famed Spitfire and better than any German fighter. When the United States installed additional fuel tanks in the P-51 it could easily fly escort missions deep into Germany.

By 1944 the "Pea Shooter" was escorting the heavy bombers all the way to Berlin and back and knocking the German *Luftwaffe* out of the sky in great numbers. By the end of the war the P-51 could fly further without refueling than the B-17 Flying Fortress!

And now in this new war the "Pea Shooter" was again proving itself a great aid to the Allied cause. Only this time it was flying and fighting not just for Great Britain and the United States, the two nations that had developed the famed fighter, but in the name of all of the United Nations.

The veteran pilots of the 5th Air Force in Korea did much joking about their own age as well as that of their planes.

"We're the best bunch of bald-headed tigers the Air Force has ever seen," they said.

Bald-headed or not, they helped turn the tide of battle along the Pusan perimeter by strafing troops and supply lines and bombing roads and key communications centers, both by day and during the long, dark Korean nights.

By mid-August General Walker's 8th Army had been further strengthened by the arrival of the United States

2nd Infantry Division, the 1st Marine Brigade, the 5th Regimental Combat Team from Hawaii, and four battalions of medium tanks. Several ROK divisions were also being reorganized to aid the ROK divisions that were already defending the northern front, and by the end of the month Great Britain's 27th Infantry Brigade would reach Korea from Hong Kong. These 1,500 British soldiers were the first combat troops other than those of the United States to join the U.N. forces.

It was the arrival of the United States Marines on August 2, however, that caused a new fighting spirit to surge through the ranks of the weary defenders. A whole division of Leathernecks had been requested, but at this time there were fewer than 90,000 men in the entire Marine Corps. Nevertheless, the vanguard of 5,000 combat-seasoned veterans swaggered ashore as if they were an entire division. The Leathernecks were self-confident to the point of being cocky.

"Everything's gonna be O.K., Mac, now that we're here," they said. "Don't worry about a thing."

This attitude annoyed some of the G.I.'s who had been in action for the past month. But the Marines had the record in two world wars to back up their cockiness, and their commander, Brigadier General Edward Craig, made it clear that he expected them to add new luster to that record in this war. Craig told his men:

"The Pusan perimeter is like a weakened dike, and we'll be used to plug holes in it as they open. It will be costly fighting against an enemy that outnumbers us." Then, after a pause, he added, "Marines have never lost a battle. This Brigade will not be the first one to do so."

By August 7, which was the eighth anniversary of the Marine landings on Guadalcanal in World War II, the Leathernecks were in the thick of the Korean fighting.

With growing fury the North Koreans struck at half a dozen places along the Pusan perimeter in their Great Naktong Offensive. These attacks were aimed at finding a weak spot through which a drive could be mounted to capture Taegu and the town of Masan, a few miles west of Pusan.

To offset the North Korean offensive against Masan, General Walker ordered a counterattack by Task Force Kean. Led by Major General William Kean, the task force was spearheaded by the Marine brigade. The Marines were not accustomed to defensive fighting. They promptly drove the enemy back more than 25 miles, relieving the threat to Masan and giving General Walker his first decisive victory of the Korean War.

In addition to Pershing tanks which were now available, the Marines also used air support very successfully in this drive. Their Corsairs, flying off the decks of the Navy carriers *Sicily* and *Badoeng Strait* in the Sea of Japan, blasted the enemy with fiery napalm, rockets and machine-gun fire.

Masan was no longer threatened but now Taegu was in serious danger. Attacking heavily in an area known as the Naktong Bulge, the North Koreans drove toward a vital railroad center at the town of Miryang. If Miryang fell, nearby Taegu would be isolated. At this point General Walker again ordered the Marines into fire-brigade action.

Watching the Marines march off to battle, a British military observer sent the following dispatch to his commanders in Tokyo on August 16:

"The situation is critical and Miryang may be lost. The enemy has driven a division-sized salient across the Naktong. More will cross the river tonight. If Miryang is lost Taegu be-

comes untenable and we will be faced with a withdrawal from Korea. I am heartened that the Marine Brigade will move against the Naktong salient tomorrow. They are faced with impossible odds, and I have no valid reason to substantiate it, but I have a feeling they will halt the enemy.

"I realize my expression of hope is unsound, but these Marines have the swagger, confidence, and hardness that must have been in Stonewall Jackson's Army of the Shenandoah. They remind me of the Coldstreams at Dunkirk. Upon this thin line of reasoning, I cling to the hope of victory."

When the Marines attacked the Naktong Bulge, they were not at all sure where in South Korea they were. Many of the maps with which they had been supplied were faulty, and most of the names on the maps were impossible to pronounce. The key ridge they were ordered to assault was apparently labelled Obong-ni.

"The devil with that," a sergeant said. "It's No-Name Ridge. Now let's go take it."

They did. Once again supported by the gull-winged Corsairs that dove down almost to ground level to drop their bombs, the Leathernecks advanced against withering enemy fire. Twice they were hurled back on the first day, but by that night a slim line of men had gained the summit. The next day they attacked in force again and completely routed the North Koreans.

The Marines did not stop their drive with the spectacular capture of No-Name Ridge. Led by Corsair air strikes, they drove the enemy all the way to the Naktong River. More than 4,000 North Korean dead were counted on the battlefield, and in the enemy's attempt to get back across the Naktong so many were killed that the river literally ran red with blood.

Little sympathy was felt for the North Koreans, however, as evidences of their atrocities were discovered. Not only did they shoot captured civilians they suspected of being sympathetic to the United Nations, but they also bound and shot American G.I.'s. On August 17 a U.S. infantry regiment recaptured one enemy position and found the bodies of 26 G.I.'s who had had their hands tied behind their backs before they were machine-gunned to death. Similar discoveries were made all through the war. They caused General MacArthur to issue a stern warning to the North Korean military leaders that he would personally hold them responsible for their criminal actions in shooting prisoners of war.

Early in September six North Korean divisions were hurled at the United States 2nd and 25th Infantry Divisions. Once again the 5th Air Force was called on to halt the enemy's desperate bid to establish a breakthrough. A few days later General Kean said, "The close air support given us by the 5th Air Force saved us as they have many times before."

The constant long-range hammering at the enemy's supply lines by the Air Force was also beginning to produce dramatic results. In each battle the North Koreans continued to use their human-sea method of attacking in several infantry waves in an effort to overwhelm the defenders, but there was now a definite difference. In an assault against the 2nd Division on September 9 the first enemy waves were armed. The last waves came in unarmed, with orders to pick up rifles and grenades from the dead and wounded on the battlefield.

Meanwhile, General MacArthur told General Walker he would have to release the Marines that had been assigned to him so they could be used for a new offensive that the United Nations commander was planning. Walker did not want to release the Leathernecks. He, like most of the officers under MacArthur, was opposed to the new offensive. Nevertheless, the Marines were withdrawn from the beachhead.

General MacArthur was a living legend. He had already gained undying fame as a hero in two world wars. But the great American war leader was to reach the very peak of his military genius at this point in the Korean conflict with his daring plan for an amphibious landing at Inchon. One of the greatest counter-blows in the history of warfare, the Inchon landing would free the entire southern half of the Korean peninsula in one mighty stroke.

Four

"Handicaps?
Inchon's
Got
'Em All!"

"We've drawn up a list of every possible handicap for an amphibious operation," a high ranking U.S. Navy officer told General MacArthur, "and Inchon's got 'em all!"

"Nevertheless that's where we're going to land," Mac-Arthur said firmly. "And I'll tell you why. The enemy has the bulk of his troops fighting along the Pusan perimeter. He has no defense at Inchon. He won't expect us there because he thinks nobody would be foolish enough to try such an operation. When we seize Inchon and recapture Seoul, it will destroy the enemy supply lines and seal off South Korea. Without supplies, the North Koreans at Pusan will be paralyzed."

The Navy officer shook his head. What MacArthur said was true enough — *if* they could land at Inchon. But it was a mighty big if.

Inchon, 20 miles from Seoul, was South Korea's second largest port. Among the many drawbacks to making a landing there were Inchon's tremendous tides, which were the world's second highest. Their average rise and fall was more than 20 feet. On September 15, the date MacArthur had picked for the invasion, the rise and fall would be at least 30 feet according to naval charts.

The ebbs and flow of the Inchon waters were also swift. The tides raced as fast as seven miles an hour through "Flying Fish Channel," which was the main approach to the port. Once high tide was reached, low tide took place so quickly that boats could be stranded on the harbor's mud flats in a matter of minutes. A ship stranded in the channel would block the way for all other landing craft.

It would not be only the landing craft that might become "sitting ducks" for the enemy shore batteries. The Navy had no recent charts of the area, and it was feared that heavy bombardment ships might stray into unmarked channels and also be grounded in the mud and ooze.

As a final argument against the Inchon landings, the Marines who were to lead the assault objected to the fact that their "beachhead" was actually in the middle of a city of a quarter of a million people. They would have to land in a port area where the sea wall, warehouses and supply sheds could conceal thousands of enemy troops.

MacArthur stubbornly held to his plan despite all of these objections — and despite the fact that he had not yet had final approval on it from the Joint Chiefs of Staff in Washington. When he did hear from Washington, it was not the word he was hoping for. The message said that General J. Lawton Collins, Army Chief of Staff, and Admiral Forrest Sherman, Chief of Naval Operations, were on their way to Tokyo to talk with him about Inchon. MacArthur knew they were going to try and talk him out of it.

All during his Army career MacArthur had been known as a daring officer. Some people had even called him foolhardy. But it had been his dashing approach to military operations that had so often been the very reason for their success. In many ways he took after his father, Arthur MacArthur, who had been an Army officer during the Civil War and later spent almost a quarter of a century fighting Indians. Arthur MacArthur was called "the Boy Colonel of the West" and was awarded the Congressional Medal of Honor. His son Douglas also gained military fame at an early age and received America's highest award for valor in battle.

Douglas MacArthur was born on January 26, 1880, at the military barracks at Little Rock, Arkansas. He attended military school as a boy and entered West Point in 1899. He was graduated four years later with a scholastic average of 98.14, the highest of any student in 25 years.

His first service as an Army officer was in the Philippines, where his father had also served. Shortly after the Russo-Japanese War he acted as an aide to his father, who was an American military observer in Tokyo. This father son team was formed when President Theodore Roosevelt asked his Secretary of War, William Howard Taft, who were the best men for the job.

"There are just two," Taft said, "and they're both named MacArthur."

Later young MacArthur was also an aide to President Roosevelt. When World War I began he was a major.

In October 1917 MacArthur was sent to France with the famous Rainbow Division which he had helped organize. Later he became its commander — the youngest division commander in the army. As an infantry colonel and then a brigadier general, he rapidly gained fame as "the most daring officer in the A.E.F." He made his head quarters within a few yards of the front lines and, dressed in an enlisted man's uniform, he took part in raids to capture German prisoners. He received two wounds and was severely gassed. He was awarded 13 decorations, received numerous other citations for bravery under fire and was praised by the French for his brilliant staff work.

After the Armistice was signed, MacArthur was named Superintendent of West Point. He then served at various military posts and in 1925 was a member of the court-martial board that found General William "Billy" Mitchell guilty of insubordination. Mitchell had been Chief of the Air Service in World War I and wanted the peace-time Army to adopt his advanced theories about the use of bombers in warfare. His public statements on the subject led to his trial. It was rumored that General MacArthur voted to acquit Mitchell, but the individual decisions of the courtmartial board were never made public. When MacArthur became the youngest Army Chief of Staff in history in 1930, he adopted many of Mitchell's air power ideas.

General MacArthur married Jean Marie Faircloth, a wealthy young woman from Tennessee, on April 30, 1937. They had one child, a son Arthur, who was born in February 1938. His father called him "The Sergeant."

The year of his marriage MacArthur retired from the army at the age of 57. He retired, he said, "to make room for the promotion of younger officers." At the time he was serving as the head of a military advisory commission in the Philippines. One of the members of his staff was a young major named Dwight D. Eisenhower. Neither MacArthur nor Eisenhower realized that within a few short years each would be commanding separate theaters of war in the greatest conflict the world had ever seen.

General MacArthur was recalled to active duty in the

summer of 1941 on the eve of America's entry into World War II. When the Japanese attacked Pearl Harbor, he was put in charge of the United States forces in the Far East. There then began a long, tragic series of American defeats in the Pacific. The Philippines fell after a bitter siege — a siege, however, that upset the Japanese military timetable for conquest. MacArthur's brilliant efforts in conducting this delaying action earned him the Medal of Honor, the decoration his father had been awarded half a century earlier.

Before the final fall of the Philippines, MacArthur and his family were ordered by President Franklin D. Roosevelt to escape to Australia. Arriving in Australia, MacArthur declared, "I came through, and I shall return!" The defiant statement became a rallying cry for the Allies in the Pacific as they stopped the Japanese advances and then began their own offensive that took them to the doorstep of Japan. MacArthur kept his promise to return when he waded ashore at Leyte Gulf in October 1944.

After accepting the Japanese surrender aboard the *U.S.S. Missouri* in Tokyo Bay on September 2, 1945, MacArthur — a five-star general now — became occupation commander of Japan. The Japanese had always respected him as a military leader, and their respect for him grew as a civil administrator. He started many legal and political reforms in an effort to introduce a more democratic way of life into Japan. He also encouraged the growth of democracy in Korea and worked with Military Governor William Dean toward the establishment of the Republic of Korea with Syngman Rhee as its first president.

These dreams of establishing a stronghold of freedom and democracy in the Far East had been all but shattered with the military invasion of South Korea by the North Korean Communists. General MacArthur knew the dreams would be completely destroyed unless the United

Nations could win this war and win it quickly. A long, drawn-out war would not only be costly in lives but would cause the free nations of the West to lose face in the Orient. He did not want to see this happen right at the time when much of the Far East was beginning to believe in democracy in action as they had seen it practiced in South Korea and Japan. And the quickest way to win this war, he was absolutely convinced, was by invading the Korean peninsula at Inchon.

Nine generals and admirals sat down at the conference table in Tokyo's Dai Ichi building, which was the U.N. commander's headquarters, to discuss the Inchon landings. MacArthur sat calmly puffing his corncob pipe as General Collins presented the Army's objections — all of which MacArthur had already carefully considered.

"Even if you do recapture Seoul," Collins concluded, "are you certain Walker's forces can break out of the perimeter and make contact with you in the north?"

MacArthur nodded. "Absolutely certain," he said quietly. "We'll have the North Korean army in a gigantic anvil and hammer situation. Our forces at Seoul will be the anvil against which Walker's army can strike. The amphibious landing is the most powerful tool we have. To use it properly we must hit hard and deep into enemy territory and cut his supply lines. I don't have to tell you gentlemen that the history of war proves that in nine cases out of ten an army has been destroyed because its supply lines have been severed."

"What about Wolmi-do?" Admiral Sherman asked. Wolmi-do was a fortified island in the harbor that guarded the approach to Inchon. (In the Korean language "-do" means island.)

MacArthur smiled. He and Sherman had been through many dark days together during World War II. "The Navy and Marines have never let me down yet," he said.

"I have confidence that they can take Wolmi-do quickly just before we land at Inchon. As a matter of fact, I seem to have more confidence in them than they have in me."

But Collins and Sherman and their aides were not to be put off. They agreed that an amphibious landing should be made, but why at an impossible place like Inchon? Why not at Pyongyang, the North Korean capital, or Kunsan? There were at least actual beaches there on which LST's (landing ship, tank) could land.

"Pyongyang is too far above the 38th parallel and thus too far from the battlefront to be effective," MacArthur said. "Kunsan is too far south and thus too close to the Pusan perimeter. If we landed at Kunsan we wouldn't trap the North Korean army. It would just retreat a few miles and we'd be back where we started from. No, gentlemen, it *must* be Inchon." His final words were hard with challenge — a challenge which no one in the room seemed to want to accept.

Then, in a friendlier tone, MacArthur added, "If I'm wrong and the first men ashore run into too much of a defense, I'll order them to withdraw. The only serious loss in that case will be my reputation. But Inchon will *not* fail. It will succeed — and it will save a quarter of a million casualties." His final words were similar to those he had spoken in the dark days of World War II. "We shall land at Inchon," he said, "and I shall crush them."

A few days later General MacArthur's plan was approved by the Joint Chiefs of Staff.

Before the landings actually began, Navy planners wanted more on-the-spot information about the Inchon harbor defenses. The only way to get this information was to send in a man on an intelligence mission. The officer chosen for this dangerous job was Lieutenant Eugene Franklin Clark.

Lieutenant Clark was ideally suited for his assignment. An ex-enlisted man who had served in the Pacific during World War II, Clark had lived in the Orient after the war and spoke Japanese and Chinese. He was familiar with the types of people he would find on the offshore islands of Inchon and knew he could make friends with them. To make certain of a friendly reception, he took along a boatload of food and other supplies. He was also equipped with a radio.

On a dark night some two weeks before the invasion, Lieutenant Clark was put ashore on the island of Yonghung-do, about 10 miles from Inchon. The next day he sought out the mayor of the island and explained his mission. The mayor immediately agreed to help Clark as much as possible, offering him a small "army" of 150 boys ranging in age from 14 to 18. Clark called his boys' army "the Young Men's Association."

Some of the members of the Young Men's Association were assigned to guard duty, to give warning if any enemy boats approached Yonghung-do. Others were sent to the island of Wolmi-do to count the number of heavy guns, and still others were assigned the task of measuring the exact height of the sea walls in Inchon harbor. Clark immediately radioed this valuable information back to his superior officers.

Clark himself rowed into Inchon harbor at night to test the mud flats. While in the harbor, he discovered the small island of Palmi-do on which there was a searchlight that had served as a beacon before the war. The Communists had put it out of commission, but Clark carefully inspected the light and felt certain that he could get it back in working order in time for the invasion, which was now about to begin.

On the calm, sunny morning of September 13, 1950,

the pre-invasion naval attack began as 10 United Nations warships steamed boldly into Inchon harbor. Six destroyers led two American and two British cruisers right under the shore guns of the enemy. The purpose of this maneuver was to get the North Koreans to fire on the U.N. ships and thus reveal the defensive gun positions which Clark's boys' army had counted with complete accuracy. (After the invasion all of the information the boys had gathered proved equally accurate). The maneuver worked. Within a matter of minutes the shore batteries on Wolmi-do opened up. As soon as they did, carrier planes from ships out in the Yellow Sea swept the island with rockets and napalm bombs. Heavy guns from the destroyers and cruisers also smashed at the enemy's shore batteries. The next day the defenses were again battered by air and sea bombardment.

On September 15, the day of the Inchon landings, some 261 ships were available to MacArthur. Seven nations — Australia, Britain, Canada, France, Holland, South Korea and the United States — were represented, although most of the forces were American.

It had been part of the original plan to have the battleship *Missouri* on hand to support the invasion troops with its 16-inch long-range guns. MacArthur had felt that the presence of the "Mighty Mo," on whose decks the Japanese had surrendered at the end of World War II, would be a good omen. But there was some doubt that the big battleship could arrive in time. While the invasion was still in the planning stages, the *Missouri* had been threatened by a hurricane in North American waters off Cape Hatteras. Later it had barely escaped a severe tropical storm off Panama.

"Don't worry," Vice Admiral Arthur Struble told MacArthur, "the *Missouri* will be here." Struble was the naval commander of the expedition.

"At Inchon? You're sure?"

Struble smiled. He had sided with Admiral Sherman in questioning the wisdom of the invasion and was especially worried about his ships getting stuck in the mud banks of the harbor. But once the expedition had been given the green light, Struble was determined to make it succeed. Now he suddenly remembered that just last January the Mighty Mo had gone aground on a mud bank in Chesapeake Bay.

"Sure I'm sure," Admiral Struble said. "You know how much the *Missouri* likes mud."

In the final planning stages of the operation it was decided to use the *Missouri* as a decoy. The ship was known to everyone in the Orient, and to fool the North Koreans into expecting a landing at a point other than Inchon, the *Missouri* stood offshore near Samchok on the opposite side of the peninsula and hurled its shells into the city. Later it was used to support the ground troops breaking out of the Pusan perimeter.

The actual invasion began before dawn. As the invasion fleet came cruising up Flying Fish Channel, sailors and marines were amazed to see the beacon on Palmi-do brightly guiding their way. Atop the lighthouse, a blanket wrapped around his weary shoulders, Lieutenant Eugene Clark now sat resting and waiting, his work done and the flashing searchlight signalling his success.

The U.S. Marines stormed ashore on Wolmi-do island at 6:30 A.M. The Marine brigade was built up to division strength now. It would be followed ashore at Inchon by the U.S. Army 7th Infantry Division, which had been training in Japan.

Opposition on Wolmi-do was light. What few defenders there were had been stunned by the air and sea bombardment. Less than an hour after they landed, the Leathernecks ran up the American flag on one of Wolmi-do's high hills and a message was sent to MacArthur aboard his flagship, the *Mount McKinley:*

MARINES HAVE TAKEN WOLMI-DO!

MacArthur immediately radioed Admiral Struble:

NEVER HAVE THE NAVY AND MARINES
SHOWN SO BRIGHTLY AS THIS MORNING!

That evening at 5:30 P.M., as a blood-red sun went burning down, the invasion of Inchon itself began. The Marines landed at two so-called "beaches," which were actually sections of the dark, 15-foot-high stone sea wall that belted the Harbor. The assault areas were called Red Beach and Blue Beach. In charge of the men assigned to Blue Beach was Colonel Lewis B. "Chesty" Puller, a legendary marine who was often called "the toughest man in the Corps." He had won more medals than any other marine in history — 50 of them, including the Navy Cross with which he had been decorated five times.

Puller had been a corporal in World War I and had earned a battlefield commission. Hard faced, barrel chested, bandy-legged Puller had continued his heroic feats on Guadalcanal in World War II. In one engagement he had been hit by numerous shell fragments and rifle fire. Doctors dug out several pieces of shrapnel and were just about to remove another from his thigh when he realized that if they did so he would be out of combat for several weeks.

"When I was a kid," he said, "I saw old Civil War soldiers walking around my home town with enough iron in them to start a junk yard. Leave that one hunk of iron in my leg." A week later he was back in action.

Now he told his men who were about to assault Inchon,

72

United States Marines raise the American flag on Wolmi-do within an hour after storming ashore to capture the island in Inchon's harbor. (Defense Department Photo — Marine Corps)

The Inchon landing was one of the great amphibious counter-blows in military history. The "beachhead" was actually in the heart of the city of Inchon. Marines had to use hooked ladders to scale the sea walls. (Defense Department Photo — Marine Corps)

"We're the luckiest guys in Marine Corps history. There was a time when a professional soldier had to wait 25 years between wars. We only had to wait five years for this one."

Puller's attitude was typical of the spirit shared by all of the Leathernecks who landed just a few hours before darkness in the heart of enemy-held Inchon. It was a spirit that seemed to be catching. One sailor named John Taylor who heard Puller's words left his tug in the harbor, managed to find a Marine uniform and went ashore with the assault troops. Taylor liked the Marines and his adopted brothers-in-arms liked him, but the Navy took a rather dim view of his unofficial transfer from one service to another. The Marines finally had to send him back to his tug to keep him from being charged with desertion.

Twenty-three waves of LVT's (landing vehicle, tracked) and eight LST's hit Red Beach in the gathering dark. Twenty-one waves of landing craft hit Blue Beach. The men in the first wave were equipped with hooked scaling ladders which were designed to catch on top of the sea wall. In some cases the ladders worked, in others they did not. When the ladders failed, the men hoisted one another up over the wall.

The first waves met only light and scattered fire, but then the enemy defenses stiffened and the marines began to take their first casualties. Gun smoke, dust and the haze of twilight began to hide the action. Nevertheless, the landing craft continued to smash head on into the sea wall and more and more marines fought their way ashore.

One platoon led by Lieutenant Baldomero Lopez met especially heavy fire from the enemy entrenched behind the sea wall. Lopez pulled the pin on a grenade and prepared to hurl it at a defensive bunker. Just as he raised his arm he was hit in the shoulder by rifle fire, and the live grenade fell out of his hand.

74

"Grenade!" he shouted at his men. But they stood frozen.

Lopez tried desperately to reach the explosive, but his shattered arm prevented him from doing so. Finally, like a football player falling on a fumble, he heroically threw himself on the grenade just as it exploded. Lieutenant Lopez was killed, but his self-sacrifice saved his men. He was one of 42 marines to be awarded the Congressional Medal of Honor in the Korean War. He was one of 12 marines, three of them officers and nine enlisted men, who earned the award for smothering grenades with their own bodies to protect their comrades.

As the assault waves began to move inland, Vice Admiral Struble ordered the barge in which he was commanding the naval forces to move in close to the beaches. With him in the boat was a newspaperman. Just as they neared the sea wall, a Marine private shouted:

"Get that boat out of here, you stupid jerk! We're gonna blow up this section of the sea wall!"

Struble ordered the boat to back off. Then Struble said to the newspaperman, "Which one of us do you think that marine was calling a jerk?"

Whole sections of the sea wall had now disappeared as the assault forces placed and exploded large charges of dynamite against it. More landing ships bearing vital supplies also arrived, making it possible for the Marines to continue their attack inland.

As darkness fell the tide receded rapidly, and no more landings could be made until the following morning. The enemy was on the run, however, and by the next day the reinforced ground forces were five miles inland. By September 17, the Army's 7th Infantry Division had also arrived, and the Air Force cut off all enemy attempts to get relief troops to Inchon. Kimpo Airfield, vital for landing and refueling planes to give close air support to the advancing ground troops, was also captured. The success of the entire Inchon operation was now certain.

Messages of congratulation began to pour into MacArthur's headquarters in Japan. One of them was from retired Admiral William F. "Bull" Halsey, World War II naval hero of the Pacific fighting. Typical of many messages that the U.N. commander received, Halsey's wire called MacArthur's feat: "The most masterly and daring stroke in all military history."

The fall of Seoul, after bitter last-ditch fighting, was announced on September 26, although fighting continued in the city for several days. Meanwhile, General Walker's 8th Army had smashed its way out of its beachhead and began to sweep northward, covering more than 100 miles in three days. Advance elements of Walker's 1st Cavalry Division contacted the Inchon invaders near Suwon on September 26. Thus, 32 years to the very day from the launching of General John J. Pershing's famed Meuse-Argonne drive to win World War I, MacArthur's Inchon operation defeated the North Korean Communists in this new conflict, preventing World War III. In just three months MacArthur had turned dark defeat in Korea into shining victory.

On September 29 MacArthur and his aides met with representatives of the Republic of South Korea in the recaptured capital of Seoul. There, in the blackened and battle-scarred capitol building, the ROK government was once again turned over to the old crusader for freedom, Syngman Rhee. When the ceremony was ended, General MacArthur, who had served half a century as a soldier but had never grown cynical about God or mankind in all of that time, humbly asked the assembled group to stand and join him in the Lord's Prayer. Tears streaked Syngman

Rhee's face, and he had great difficulty in expressing his thanks for his country's deliverance once again from the hands of a ruthless invader from out of the north.

By September 30 more than 130,000 enemy troops had been captured, and the North Korean army no longer existed as an organized fighting force below the 38th parallel. MacArthur asked for and was given permission by the Joint Chiefs of Staff to pursue the broken enemy forces beyond the 38th parallel to the northern border of the country, the Yalu River.

One war in Korea was now ended, but the pursuit of the North Koreans beyond the 38th parallel was to start a brand new war. Within a matter of weeks, fresh Communist armies would come streaming across the Yalu River from out of the vast wastes of China, and once again the United States and its supporting United Nations forces would meet tragic defeat.

Five

*"Home
for
Christmas!"*

On October 1, 1950, General MacArthur broadcast a demand that North Korea surrender. The North Koreans did not reply, but Mao Tse-tung, the dictator of Communist China, did. He said:

"The Chinese will not allow foreign aggression! We will not stand aside if the imperialist nations of the West invade our neighbor!"

On October 7 General Walker's 8th Army began to cross the 38th parallel.

On October 15 a high-level American policy conference was held on Wake Island in the Pacific. Those attending the meeting included President Truman; the chairman of the Joint Chiefs of Staff, General Omar Bradley; the State

Department's Dean Rusk; General MacArthur, and several aides.

"In your opinion," President Truman asked General MacArthur, "is there any chance that the Chinese might enter the war on the side of North Korea?"

MacArthur shook his head. "I'd say there's very little chance of that happening. They have several hundred thousand men north of the Yalu, but they haven't any air force. If they tried to cross the river our air force would slaughter them. At the most perhaps 60,000 troops would make it. Our infantry could easily contain them. I expect the actual fighting in North Korea to end by Thanksgiving. We should have our men home, or at least in Japan, by Christmas."

At the very moment that President Truman and General' MacArthur were talking, there were already more than 100,000 Chinese Communist troops in North Korea, and another 200,000 were ready to cross the Yalu. By mid-November at least 300,000 Chinese would be poised to strike — and the ROK, American and other U.N. forces would not even be aware of their presence. Before the war was over, the Chinese Communist armies in Korea would reach a peak strength of more than a million men.

The Chinese Red hordes that were preparing to destroy the U.N. ground troops were tough and battle-hardened from almost a quarter of a century of constant warfare. Founded in 1927, the Chinese Communist Army fought Chiang Kai-shek's Nationalist Army for the control of China in a war that raged for years. Finally, in 1934, Chiang's Nationalists cornered about 140,000 Communists in an area southwest of Shanghai. The Reds managed to fight their way out of this circle and retreat some 6,000 miles across most of China to an area southwest of Peking. This historic "Long March" was one of history's epic military feats. It would be roughly equal to an army marching from Mexico to Alaska.

The Long March lasted a little longer than a year. The Reds fought their way through 12 provinces, across countless flooded rivers and steep mountains, through blazing heat and freezing cold. They averaged about 15 miles a day, despite the fact that many of them were barefoot. Of the 140,000 who started on the Long March, only about 20,000 were left when it ended.

The survivors soon began to increase the size of their army. Within 15 years, including a time-out period during World War II when it fought against the Japanese, this army was able to drive Chiang's Nationalists off the continent to the island of Formosa. It was this same army, with its hard core of veterans of the Long March, that now threatened the United Nations forces in North Korea.

The reason the Chinese Communists were able to cross the Yalu without being detected was because in their long years of warfare they had learned that hiding their movements was literally a life-and-death matter. They traveled only by night, yet between darkness and dawn they could march almost 20 miles. As soon as it grew light, every soldier, weapon and pack animal was hidden in nearby forests or villages. If any soldier showed himself by day, he was promptly shot. Thus, although U.N. aircraft constantly patrolled the Yalu River, no Chinese were seen or photographed.

Nevertheless, advance U.N. ground troops did begin to capture an occasional enemy who spoke neither Korean nor Japanese. Intelligence officers decided that these prisoners must be Chinese "volunteers," and not part of an organized Chinese invasion force. Even when the U.S. 1st

Cavalry Division was hit by a powerful Chinese attack on November 1 and lost some 600 men, MacArthur and his aides refused to believe that the situation was deadly serious. After all, MacArthur reasoned, the U.N. still had absolute control of the air and with such air power an invasion could easily be smashed. Here too the U.N. commander was to be fooled. Fortunately, however, when the Chinese Communist air force did suddenly strike it would be badly defeated by superior American flyers and superior American planes.

In his talk with President Truman, MacArthur had said the Chinese had no air force. This was true, in a sense, but he did not take into consideration the fact that Russia was ready, willing and able to supply its Red allies with the latest types of jet aircraft and even train Chinese pilots to fly these up-to-date combat planes.

Early in November several enemy jet fighter planes were seen south of the Yalu. They were identified as Russian-built MIG-15's. On November 8 the first jet plane combat in history took place between United States Air Force F-80 Shooting Stars and MIG-15's. In the aerial fight a MIG was shot down by Lieutenant Russell Brown. This first jet "kill" of the Korean War proved to be a good omen for the U.N. flyers and a bad omen for the Reds.

The F-80 Shooting Star was later replaced in Korea by the F-84 Thunderjet, a fighter-bomber. The American plane that gained fame as the "MIG Killer" was the F-86 Sabrejet. This ship knocked MIG's out of the sky at a 14-to-1 rate during the entire course of the war. Between 823 and 839 MIG's were shot down during the conflict. Some 800 of these were destroyed by Sabrejets with a loss of 59 of the F-86's.

There were 40 American flyers who shot down five or

Sleek U.S. Air Force F-86 Sabrejets patrol "MIG Alley" in Northwest Korea. (U.S. Air Force Photo)

Captain Joseph McConnell, with 16 aerial victories, was the top jet ace in Korea. (U.S. Air Force Photo)

Major James Jabara, the first jet ace. (U.S. Air Force Photo)

more planes to become aces in the air war over Korea. Captain Joseph McConnell with 16 victories was the top jet ace. He also became the first "triple jet ace" in history when he shot down three MIG's in one day — May 18, 1953. Major James Jabara became the first jet ace on May 20, 1951. His final score was 15 enemy planes, a record second only to McConnell's. The Marine Corps' first jet ace was Sabrejet pilot Major John F. Bolt, who shot down half a dozen MIG's while temporarily assigned to the Air Force.

Lieutenant Guy Pierre Bordelon was the only Navy pilot to shoot down five enemy planes in Korea. Late in the war he was temporarily assigned to the 5th Air Force to combat night bombing attacks by the Reds. The single-engined planes used by the Reds for these night raids flew so slowly that jet aircraft were unable to maneuver quickly enough to shoot them down. Although these night raids did no major damage, they did affect the morale of the ground troops, who called the raiders "Bed Check Charlies." Flying a radar-equipped, propeller-driven Corsair, Lieutenant Bordelon shot down two YAK's on June 30, 1953, two more Bed Check Charlies on July 5 and a final one on July 16.

Four United States Air Force heroes were awarded the Congressional Medal of Honor for their heroic exploits in Korea. All four men died in earning their awards. They were Major Louis J. Sebille, an F-51 Mustang pilot; Major George A. Davis, Jr., an F-86 Sabrejet pilot; Major Charles J. Loring, Jr., an F-80 Shooting Star pilot, and Captain John S. Walmsley, Jr., pilot of a B-26 bomber.

These four made a total of 47 flyers to be awarded the Medal of Honor since Lieutenant Frank Luke had won the first one awarded an American airman for shooting down 18 or 19 balloons and aircraft in 17 days in France during World War I. Sabrejet pilot George Davis performed a similar feat. He destroyed a dozen Red planes in 16 days before he himself was shot down.

Major Sebille and Major Loring earned their awards in separate actions when they deliberately dived their crippled planes into enemy anti-aircraft batteries. Sebille was the first Air Force Medal of Honor winner in the Korean War.

Many flyers said that Medals of Honor should have been awarded all of the pilots of the veteran B-26's for their noble service "above and beyond the call of duty" in Korea. Captain Walmsley had his old B-26 fitted with a special searchlight for use on night missions. On one such bombing and strafing attack his crew used up all of their ammunition before the target was destroyed. Walmsley contacted a sister ship and told its pilot he would guide him in by lighting up the target with his searchlight. The target was destroyed, but Walmsley's plane was crippled by anti-aircraft fire. The heroic pilot ordered his crew to bail out, and moments later the plane exploded.

In one important way the air war in Korea was a strange one. Even when it became perfectly clear that the Chinese Communists had entered the war, the U.N. air force was not allowed to fly north of the Yalu River. The United Nations, President Truman and the Joint Chiefs of Staff felt that an attack beyond the Yalu might bring Russia into the conflict and start World War III. With Manchuria thus placed "off limits," the airfields that housed the MIG-15's and the supply depots that supported the Communist armies could not be bombed.

American fighter pilots were especially irritated by the Yalu River "fence" which they were ordered not to cross.

When they met enemy fighters in combat, the MIG's often fled beyond the Yalu as soon as they began to lose the fight. American radar and radio controllers kept careful track of U.N. fighter planes, and as soon as they neared the Yalu they were warned away. In describing one such incident an American Sabrejet pilot said:

"There I was on that MIG's tail. I didn't care where I was. All I wanted to do was get that MIG. Then guess what happened? That blasted controller called me off. 'Calling Blue Leader, calling Blue Leader,' he radioed. 'You're on the fence. Uncle Sam won't like that. Be a good little boy now, and come home.' So I came back. Even a fighter pilot doesn't have any privacy these days. Everybody wants to get into the act."

From the outbreak of the Korean War until the truce was signed, control of the air was vital to the success of the U.N. forces. Lieutenant General George E. Stratemeyer, commander of the United States Far East Air Forces, summed it up when he said, "The Korean War again proves the basic fact that air superiority must be won before ground and sea forces can move freely in modern war."

Nevertheless, it was the infantry that bore the brunt of the fighting in Korea. It was the common foot soldiers who decided the outcome of countless grim battles in the barren hills. And it was the ground troops — the G.I.'s and Marines who proudly answered to the nicknames of "dog faces" and "squareheads" — who took the greatest losses. Of the approximately 34,000 United States battle deaths about 28,000 were suffered by the Army and more than 4,000 by the Marines, as compared with 1,200 Air Force and about 450 Navy men killed in action. The roll call of the wounded told the same story. This was an infantryman's war. Some 77,000 Army men and about 23,000 Marines were wounded as against 1,500 Navy and about 350 Air Force wounded.

Since General Walker was officially in charge of all U.N. and ROK ground troops in Korea, he took it for granted that when the advance into North Korea began the ROK Army, the U.S. 8th Army, and the Army and Marine divisions that had made the Inchon landings would be under his single unified command. General MacArthur decided to keep the commands divided, however. Walker continued to lead the 8th Army and the ROK forces, while the Inchon invaders (the 1st Marine and 7th Army Divisions) were commanded by Major General Edward Almond. Almond's forces were called the 10th Corps.

Soon after the recapture of Seoul, MacArthur told Walker that General Almond's troops were to be used for another amphibious landing at Wonsan on the east coast of Korea. From there they would drive west toward Pyongyang, the North Korean capital, while Walker's troops drove toward the same goal from the south. This meant that the 1st Marine Division had to board ships at Inchon, sail around the lower tip of the peninsula and then up the east coast to make the assault. The 7th Army Division was ordered to move overland to Pusan where it was to board ships and sail for Wonsan. By the time the 7th Division had embarked, however, Wonsan was already captured, and the division was ordered to make an amphibious landing further up the coast at Iwon. This operation took place against little opposition.

The Marines were also too late to take part in the capture of Wonsan. When they arrived at their destination, South Korean ground units known as the "Rambling ROK's" were already in possession of the city. In addition, the harbor was so filled with Russian mines that it took a week to clear it so the Marines could land. U.S. infantry units also moved into the city while the amphibious troops sailed impatiently up and down the east coast. The Marines, disgusted because the war seemed to be passing them by, called this futile sailing back and forth "Operation Yo-Yo."

By the time the Marines were able to land, Wonsan was so safe that comedian Bob Hope and a U.S.O. entertainment troupe arrived by plane and put on a show for the G.I.'s and ROK's. This gave the G.I.'s the chance they had been looking for to even the score with the Leathernecks for their swaggering entry into Pusan earlier in the war. When the Marines finally landed they were greeted by the G.I.'s singing a new verse they had made up for the Marine Corps Hymn:

> "Those tough and fighting Gyrenes
>   Wherever they may go,
> They're always bringing up the rear
>   Behind Bob Hope and the U.S.O."

Even the Leathernecks knew when they were licked. They took the G.I.'s gibes good-naturedly. But this was to be the last bit of comedy to take place in Korea for some time to come. Before the year was ended the U.N. forces were to find themselves engaged in a grim fight for survival.

In mid-November Walker's and Almond's forces began an all-out drive toward the Yalu River and the Manchurian border. The day before Thanksgiving, the 17th Regiment of the U.S. 7th Infantry Division reached the Yalu. This was the only American unit to reach the Manchurian border during the war. On the evening of November 27 the 1st Marine Division and some units of the Army's 7th Division were suddenly hit by an overwhelming force of Chinese Communist troops near Chosen Reservoir. There then began the fierce battle of "Frozen Chosen" — one of the epic retreats in American military annals. But the Marines refused to call it a retreat.

"We're attacking in a different direction," they said.

Six

*The
Battle
of Frozen
Chosen*

"This must be the only blasted place in the world where a guy can be up to his neck in mud one day and have snow blowing in his face the next!"

This was a typical comment made by the Marine riflemen as they advanced along the narrow, mountainous road toward the Chosen Reservoir in North Korea. At Pusan in South Korea they had had to fight not only the enemy but also the hills and the terrible heat. Along the shores of the Naktong River and at Inchon Harbor, mud banks were a major problem. Early in the war the Leathernecks had also been forced to wade through rice paddies in filthy water that was literally neck deep. Now, in North Korea, the weather had completely changed. Winter was at hand with freezing blasts coming down across

89

Asia, bringing temperatures as low as 30 degrees below zero.

MacArthur's late November drive toward the Yalu was in the form of a two-pronged attack. On the left or west was the 8th Army, and on the right or east was the 10th Corps. Separating these two commands was the long, high Korean mountain range. Thus the right flank of the 8th Army and the left flank of the 10th Corps were unprotected. In addition, communications between the two commands were hampered by the 75 miles of rugged mountains that separated them.

At this time General Walker's 8th Army was made up of the following forces: the U.S. Army 1st Cavalry, 2nd, 24th and 25th Divisions, four ROK divisions, a British Commonwealth brigade, a Turkish brigade, an independent brigade and single battalions of Philippine and Thailand troops. General Almond's 10th Corps included the following: the U.S. Army 3rd and 7th Divisions, the 1st Marine Division, two ROK divisions and a small group of British Royal Marines.

In the twin drive toward the Manchurian border, the 8th Army attacked through northwest Korea, and the 10th Corps attacked through northeast Korea. Spearheading the 10th Corps drive were the 1st Division Marines. Their route took them some 80 miles along a one-lane road carved through the mountains from the port city of Hungnam to the tiny village of Yudam-ni on the western shore of the Chosen Reservoir. Along the way they marched through the villages of Hamhung, Chinhung-ni, Koto-ri and Hagaru-ri. Division headquarters were set up at Hagaru-ri. (In the Korean language "-ni" and "-ri" mean village or town.)

General Oliver Smith, commander of the 1st Marine Division, did not like this method of advancing in a long,

Three U.S. riflemen try to dry themselves around a small fire during Korea's rainy season. (U.S. Army Photograph)

thin column into unknown enemy country. Fearing a trap in the frozen mountain passes, he deliberately slowed the advance. Word had already reached him of Chinese Communist attacks that had sent the 8th Army reeling back in the west, and he expected a similar blow against his own forces at any time. But with General Almond constantly prodding him on, Smith had little choice but to order the advance to continue. He urged his officers to proceed with great caution.

General Smith's worst fears were to be realized when the 5th and 7th Marine Regiments passed west of the Chosen Reservoir and reached Yudam-ni. This was to be the signal for the enemy to strike with savage fury in an effort to destroy the 25,000 Marines strung out along the road leading back from Yudam-ni to Hungnam on the coast. The Reds' plan was to cut the vital road in several places and set up roadblocks. These roadblocks would act like dams in a stream, stopping the flow of Marines southward if they tried to escape from the trap. The enemy then intended to surround the four isolated forces at Yudam-ni, Hagaru-ri, Koto-ri and Chinhung-ni and destroy them one at a time.

"They planned on shooting us like fish in a barrel," was the way one rifleman later put it.

Keeping the road open back to Hungnam was thus to become a matter of life and death.

One key point along the road was a mountain gap midway between Yudam-ni and Hagaru-ri called Toktong Pass. When the 5th and 7th Regiments went into position at Yudam-ni on the afternoon of November 27, Captain William E. Barber's F-for-Fox Company was assigned to Toktong Pass on the nearby heights.

To Captain Barber, a regular Marine officer and a veteran of the grim Iwo Jima fighting in World War II, the

Marines of the Fifth and Seventh Regiments are shown on the icy road from Yudam-ni after hurling back a surprise attack by three Communist divisions. (Defense Department Photo — Marine Corps)

Fire and fall back! That was the order given to the Marines who were surrounded at Yudam-ni. In sub-zero weather they fought their way through Chinese hordes to Hagaru-ri on the southern tip of the Chosen Reservoir. (Defense Department Photo — Marine Corps)

pass looked like an excellent defensive position — and he had a hunch they were going to be glad it was. The 5th and 7th Regiments, he figured, were the guys who would probably get the first bloody noses, and if they got hurt badly enough they would have to fall back through this gap in the mountains. This meant that Toktong Pass absolutely *must* be held.

Captain Barber immediately posted 50 per cent of his 240-man company as perimeter guards and told the other men they could hit the sack. The off-duty men crawled into their sleeping bags eagerly enough — it was the only way they could keep from freezing to death — but they did very little sleeping even when it began to grow dark. Off in the dusk toward enemy country there was the weird sound of thousands of shuffling feet. That must be the Reds in their lousy tennis shoes getting ready to attack, the men decided. But even when the moon came out, no enemy could be seen. Finally some of the Marines were able to fall alseep.

Private Hector Cafferata awakened to the sound of blaring bugles. For a moment he thought he was back in the States lying in his sack and listening to morning reveille. He turned over inside his sleeping bag and felt a sudden draft of sub-zero air hit him. Then he remembered where he was, all right. But had he dreamed he had heard bugles? No, there they were again — and louder this time. He also heard the strange tinkling noise of cymbals being struck, and then came the sharp shrill sounds of whistles.

Cafferata was wide awake now. This must be it. The bugles and cymbals and whistles were the enemy's crazy attack signals.

"Attack! Attack!"

"Here they come!"

The alarm spread all around the perimeter now. Then

94

there was an even more chilling sound. It was voices, Chinese voices, chanting:

"We kill Marines! Marines, you die! We kill Marines! Marines, you die!"

Cafferata leaped from his sleeping bag, grabbing his rifle and praying that it would work, that its mechanism hadn't frozen solid. The M-1 worked, and Cafferata emptied it at the "gooks" who were just yards away from him. When the gun was empty, Cafferata began hurling grenades, his own and every other one he could lay his hands on.

There was a momentary lull just as Cafferata ran out of grenades, and he looked around him. He was the only man left alive in his squad. An ex-semi-professional football player back in his hometown of Boonton, New Jersey, Cafferata now brought his ability at broken-field running into play as he dashed over the snow to a nearby platoon.

The men here were almost all dead or wounded, but Cafferata found several wounded comrades who were able to load and pass him rifles. He emptied the M-1's as fast as they could be passed to him. He also hurled grenades between rifle reloadings. Several enemy grenades landed near his feet, and Cafferata either picked them up and threw them back or kicked them away. He had kicked away several grenades when he suddenly realized he was fighting in the snow in his stocking feet. He'd gotten out of his sack so fast he's forgotten his shoes! Cafferata kept on fighting.

Captain Barber had also been fighting furiously since the start of the Chinese attack. He now rallied those of his men who were still on their feet, and they tried to bring some concentrated fire to bear on the enemy. But the terrible cold proved to be as bad an enemy as the

Reds. Automatic rifles refused to work and had to be fired a shot at a time. Grenades sometimes did not explode. Mortars failed to fire. Machine guns jammed.

Again and again the thin circle of Marines had to fight hand-to-hand against the wildly yelling Chinese, killing them with bayonets, swinging rifles like baseball bats to club them off, or battling with bare fists. Even then the bitter cold took its toll. Bayonets snapped in two like frozen twigs. Rifle stocks shattered. But the Marines stood fast.

Captain Barber had his mortars firing steadily now, and as the Reds tried to bring up reserves the exploding mortar shells drove them back. Suddenly a Chinese bugle again sounded. The Reds were calling off the attack.

When dawn broke, the Marines still held Toktong Pass, and the nearby slopes were littered with more than 500 Chinese dead. Fox Company had 20 men killed and 54 wounded. Private Cafferata was one of those wounded — a grenade had torn off his little finger — but he refused to be relieved from duty. Later in the day, however, he charged an enemy machine gunner single-handed and received such a severe shoulder wound that he was forced out of action. For his heroic efforts during this engagement, Private Cafferata received the Medal of Honor.

Captain Barber was also wounded during the second day's fighting, but he refused to be evacuated. He too was to receive the Medal of Honor, one of 11 awarded to Marines in the battle of the Chosen Reservoir. That night Fox Company suffered 33 more casualties, four dead and 29 wounded, but they killed more than 200 Chinese. On the third night at Toktong Pass Captain Barber was again hit but he continued to direct the defense from a stretcher.

The unbelievably bitter cold continued to hamper the defenders. Hair tonic, which did not freeze as easily as

The Leathernecks brought their equipment, their wounded, and in some cases even their dead with them from Yudam-ni and Toktong Pass. (Defense Department Photo — Marine Corps)

Leathernecks catch a few minutes' rest during their heroic breakout from the Chosen Reservoir. (Defense Department Photo — Marine Corps)

grease, was poured on automatic weapons to keep them operating. Food and water were major problems. The men carried canteens inside their uniforms next to their bodies to keep their drinking water from freezing. Rations froze solid. By now Fox Company was down to about 80 men who could walk.

The two regiments at Yudam-ni had also been badly hit by the Chinese. It was not until December 1, however, that they decided to pull back to Hagaru-ri. When they decided to make the move, they also sent an advance party to relieve Captain Barber's company at Toktong Pass.

This relief battalion was led by Lieutenant Colonel Raymond Davis. To get to the pass, Davis and his men had to fight their way over several miles of mountainous ground that was held by the Chinese. Once again the weather was also an enemy. The men became bathed in sweat from climbing and fighting toward the mountain gap. If they rested for even a moment they were in danger of freezing to death. Colonel Davis bullied his men into staying on their feet, forced them to drive ahead despite the fact that they were already exhausted from several days of fighting. His actions saved their lives.

On the final leg of the journey the relief column floundered through waist-deep snow. There were also mountain slopes so steep and slick with ice that the men had to crawl up them on their hands and knees. Finally, at dawn on December 2, Colonel Davis contacted Captain Barber on the radio.

"Do you need help?" the severely wounded Captain Barber asked. "If you do, I can send out a patrol to meet you."

Colonel Davis looked at the Marines grouped around him. Tears were in several men's eyes at Captain Barber's brave words.

"No, thanks," Colonel Davis said over the radio. "We'll be with you in a few minutes."

Colonel Davis' men ran the rest of the way to Toktong Pass.

During the first week of December General MacArthur's headquarters in Japan had already written off as lost the Marine 1st Division and its attached Army units in Korea. In Washington the Joint Chiefs of Staff had about reached the same conclusion. But in Korea the Leathernecks and G.I.'s had just begun to fight.

By December 4 Captain Barber's Fox Company and the rest of the 5th and 7th Marine Regiments managed to make their way back from Toktong Pass and Yudam-ni to General Smith's headquarters at Hagaru-ri. An Army battalion of the 7th Division G.I.'s that had been ambushed east of the Chosen Reservoir also fought its way to the Marine division headquarters. But this did not mean that the Leathernecks and G.I.'s were safe. Hagaru-ri was also surrounded. So were the two other strongholds at Koto-ri and Chinhung-ni, which were further south on the road to the coast. Nevertheless, General Smith decided to stage a fighting breakout.

"We'll hold our present positions until the 7th Regiment clears the road to Koto-ri," the Marines were told. "Then we'll move out. When we do move out, we'll come out as Marines and not as stragglers. We're going to take our dead, wounded, and equipment when we leave. We're coming out, I tell you, as Marines or not at all."

The fighting breakout toward Koto-ri began on December 6.

At Koto-ri, Marine Colonel "Chesty" Puller was unimpressed by the apparent hopelessness of the situation. "So they've got us surrounded," he said. "That's swell. The lousy 'gooks' won't be able to get away from us this time."

Also at Koto-ri, 46-year-old Army Lieutenant Colonel John Page was waging a legendary one-man fighting campaign that helped hold the Reds at bay.

Colonel Page had been in Korea only a few days when the advance into North Korea had begun. A small, soft-spoken man who wore steel-rimmed glasses, he did not look like much of a fighter. His men knew otherwise, however. Colonel Page had a wife and two young children at home, and he wanted his children to grow up in a world that was not threatened by Communism.

"As far as I'm concerned," he said, "the Reds have to be stopped here."

Two days after the fighting had begun in the Chosen Reservoir area, Colonel Page started out from 10th Corps headquarters at Hamhung to set up radio communication stations along the road to Hagaru-ri. These stations were to be used to direct the flow of men and supplies along the vital artery. Page's jeep driver was a corporal from Macon, Georgia, David E. Klepsig.

As they neared Koto-ri, Page and Klepsig were forced off the road by a sudden attack from an enemy machine-gun crew stationed near a blown-up bridge. The two men lay hidden behind some nearby rocks for a time. Finally Colonel Page said:

"You get the jeep back on the road. I'll cover you."

Page then walked boldly toward the machine-gun crew, firing his automatic carbine, while Klepsig leaped into the jeep. A moment later Page jumped into the seat beside the corporal and they raced around the blown-up bridge, crossed the frozen river and continued to Koto-ri.

Colonel Puller's command was under heavy attack and there were already a number of casualties. Colonel Page suggested that an airstrip be built so the wounded could be evacuated to Hungnam.

"Go ahead, build it," Puller said.

Colonel Page learned that there was already a small airstrip at Koto-ri, but the runway was too short to land C-47's. It would have to be extended at least a thousand yards — a thousand yards exposed to enemy sniper fire. Nevertheless, Colonel Page rounded up some engineers, and he and a crew of volunteers went to work with trucks and graders.

When the sniper fire grew so heavy that work on the runway could not continue, Colonel Page went up in an observation plane piloted by Lieutenant Charles F. Kieffer. Kieffer flew low enough to spot the enemy sniper observation post, and Page dropped grenades on it. Page then had Kieffer continue to fly back and forth along the sniper-infested ridge so he could toss hand grenades and fire his rifle at the enemy. Soon he had killed enough of the Reds in their foxholes so that work on the airstrip could be completed. Soon more than 750 wounded men were safely flown out of Koto-ri.

But Colonel Page's most heroic feats were yet to be performed.

By the night of December 7 General Smith's forces had fought their way down the road from Hagaru-ri to join Colonel Puller's men at Koto-ri. To get there they had to slug their way through 40,000 fresh Chinese Communist troops. The next day a blizzard was blowing, but the combined forces renewed their attack toward Chinhung-ni. Mile after bitter mile along the narrow, icy road they grimly battled their way southward.

At one point the column was ambushed, and several vehicles were set aflame. These trucks completely blocked the road, and the Chinese began to pour down murderous fire on the entire column. It was here that Colonel Page performed the final heroic deeds that earned him the

Exhausted members of the First Marine Division on the road back from "Frozen Chosen." (Defense Department Photo — Marine Corps)

Elements of the First Marine Division rest on the snow-covered roadside after overcoming an ambush. (Defense Department Photo — Marine Corps)

Congressional Medal of Honor — the 78th to be awarded an Army man in Korea. Although he was an Army officer, Colonel Page was also awarded the Navy Cross for his gallant aid to the Marines. The citation for his action tells the complete story:

"Realizing the extreme danger to the stationary convoy while under the relentless fire of enemy forces commanding high ground on both sides of the road, Lieutenant Colonel Page bravely fought his way to the head of the column accompanied by a Marine private* and, undaunted by point-blank machine-gun fire, continued directly into the hostile strong-point, taking 30 of the enemy completely by surprise and inflicting severe casualties among them. With the Marine private wounded by a hand grenade fragment, Lieutenant Colonel Page ordered him to withdraw and provided him with covering fire, fiercely continuing to engage the enemy single-handedly and killing 12 of them before he himself was mortally wounded. By his valiant and aggressive fighting spirit in the face of overwhelming odds during this self-imposed mission, he was directly responsible in disrupting the hostile attack, thereby making it possible for the members of the convoy to regroup, redeploy and fight off succeeding attacks. His outstanding courage, self-sacrificing efforts and unswerving devotion to duty reflect the highest credit upon Lieutenant Colonel Page and the United States Armed Forces. He gallantly gave his life for his country."

Colonel Page's last act was not the last heroic act performed on this historic march to the sea. There were dozens of epic deeds performed by the time the Marines and G.I.'s reached the coast on December 10. And they came out of the frozen, battle-scarred hills as truly legend-

* Pfc. Marvin Wasson — D.L.

Riflemen take cover behind large boulders and engage the enemy forces who failed to trap the surrounded Marines.   (Defense Department Photo — Marine Corps)

Close air support by Marine Corsairs was a key factor in the success of the fighting breakout from the Chosen Reservoir area. Here a Corsair pilot has just dropped napalm on an enemy strongpoint.   (Defense Department Photo — Marine Corps)

ary American fighting men, bringing their supplies, their equipment, their wounded — and even their dead lashed to artillery gun barrels — with them. They had sustained almost 8,000 casualties, but they had inflicted almost 40,-000 casualties on the Chinese. It had indeed been an "attack in a different direction."

Summing up the fighting breakout from the Chosen Reservoir area and the march to the sea, Marine Commandant General Lemuel C. Shepherd said, "The opposing Chinese forces were so punished that they were no longer an immediate threat to our cause. I believe that by no stretch of the imagination can this be described as a retreat, since a retreat suggests a defeat — and the only defeat involved in the battle was the one suffered by the Chinese."

Certainly the men who had reached the sea did not regard themselves as defeated. They had not even lost their sense of humor. Recalling General MacArthur's promise, "home for Christmas," they had painted signs on their vehicles that read:

"ONLY FOURTEEN MORE SHOOTING
DAYS UNTIL CHRISTMAS!"

The Dunkirk-like evacuation of troops from Hungnam began immediately. Other 10th Corps units were also evacuated from Wonsan. By December 24 — Christmas Eve — the United States Navy had safely removed 105,-000 U.S. troops from North Korea. These fighting men were taken to South Korea, where they could prepare for a brand new war which General MacArthur was forced to tell President Truman and the Joint Chiefs of Staff had now begun.

Seven

*"Old
Soldiers
Never
Die"*

North Korea was now under the complete control of the Chinese Communists. Not only had the 10th Corps been evacuated from the east coast, but in the west the 8th Army had also been driven back below the 38th parallel.

On December 26, three days after General Walker's death, the 8th Army got a new commander. He was Lieutenant General Matthew B. Ridgeway, a famed World War II paratrooper. When he got his final instructions in Japan before he took over his new command in Korea, Ridgeway asked General MacArthur:

"If I see my way clear to renew the attack, do I have your permission to do so?"

"It's your army, Matt," MacArthur said. "You fight it the best way you know how." To prove he was giving General Ridgeway complete authority in Korea, MacArthur also placed the 10th Corps under the new 8th Army commander.

Matthew Bunker Ridgeway was born at Fort Monroe, Virginia, on March 3, 1895. His father, Colonel Thomas Ridgeway, was a career Army officer, and young Matthew grew up at various Army posts. He entered West Point in 1912, graduating in the spring of 1917 just as the United States was entering World War I. Lieutenant Ridgeway did not get overseas, however, but served with the infantry in Texas. The infantry was to remain his first love all during his career.

Between the two world wars, the tall, rugged, hawknosed Ridgeway continued his Army training at a number of posts in the United States as well as in China, Panama and the Philippines. He also advanced steadily in rank. During the period between the wars he married Margaret Wilson and their daughter, Virginia Ann, was born.

When World War II began, Major Ridgeway was serving with the War Plans Division in Washington. When the United States entered the war, he did everything possible to be assigned to a combat infantry division. When the 82nd Division — an outfit that had gained fame in World War I — became one of the first American airborne units, Ridgeway succeeded in becoming its commanding general.

General Ridgeway led the 82nd Airborne Division in the conquest of Sicily and jumped with his men in the invasion of France in June 1944. Later he commanded the 18th Airborne Corps that crossed the Rhine River on "bridges of silk" and helped end the war against Germany. He was awarded more than 30 decorations for heroism in the European fighting, including the Distinguished Service Cross and the Purple Heart.

Lieutenant General Matthew B. Ridgeway

South of Koto-ri, success is in sight as the "attack in different direction" nears Chinhung-ni and the sea. (Defense Department Photo—Marine Corps)

In addition to being an inspirational leader of combat troops, General Ridgeway was also a skilled diplomat. Before the outbreak of the Korean War he had served as an adviser to the United Nations on military matters. It was in this role that he had helped make plans for the first "international police force" — a police force like the one that was now trying to stop the Reds in Korea, and that Ridgeway himself was now being called upon to lead to victory.

When General Ridgeway took command of the 8th Army, his first statement was, "I am in Korea to stay!" There was a considerable amount of defeatism among his troops, however. Many servicemen were asking why they were in Korea. General Ridgeway answered this question with a ringing message to all of his men. Entitled "Why We Are Here," it read, in part:

"The issues are clear. It is not a question of this or that Korean town or village. Real estate is incidental. It is not restricted to the issue of freedom for our South Korean Allies, whose fidelity and valor under the severest stresses of battle we recognize; though that freedom is a symbol of the wider issues, and included among them.

"The real issues are whether the power of Western civilization, as God has permitted it to flower in our own beloved lands, shall defy and defeat Communism; whether the rule of men who shoot their prisoners, enslave their citizens, and deride the dignity of man, shall displace the rule of those to whom the individual and his individual rights are sacred; whether we are to survive with God's hand to guide and lead us, or to perish in the dead existence of a Godless world.

"If these be true, and to me they are beyond any possibility of challenge, then this has long ceased to be a fight for freedom for our Korean Allies alone and for their national sur-

vival. It has become, and it continues to be, a fight for our own freedom, for our own survival, in an honorable, independent national existence. The sacrifices we have made, and those we shall make, are not offered only for others, but in our own direct defense.

"In the final analysis, the issue now joined here in Korea is whether Communism or individual freedom shall prevail, and, make no mistake about it, whether the next flight of fear-driven people shall be checked and defeated overseas or permitted step-by-step to close in our own loved ones in all its misery and despair.

"These are the things for which we fight. Never have members of any military command had a greater challenge than we, or a finer opportunity to show ourselves and our people at their best — and thus be an honor to the profession of arms, and a credit to those who bred us."

But Ridgeway could not immediately go over to the offensive. In fact on New Year's Day 1951 the Chinese started a new drive southward, and by January 4 the South Korean capital of Seoul once again fell to the invaders. The port of Inchon also had to be evacuated in what the G.I.'s and Leathernecks described with wry humor as "an amphibious landing in reverse."

When the Chinese started their drive, MacArthur told the Joint Chiefs of Staff that unless the United Nations' policy of "limited war" were changed, the Reds could probably drive the 8th Army and its supporting forces out of Korea. To prevent this total defeat, he asked for permission to use the Far East Air Forces to bomb the Communist supply bases north of the Yalu River. This request was denied. The only action taken by the United Nations General Assembly was to adopt a resolution on February 1, 1951, that branded the People's Republic of China as an aggressor in Korea. This action was, of course, ignored by the Reds. MacArthur was then told to retreat if necessary to the former Pusan perimeter. If his losses became too great, he was authorized to withdraw his forces to Japan.

In spite of all restrictions General Ridgeway was able to rally his troops, and by the middle of March the 8th Army recaptured Seoul. This was the fourth time the city had changed hands during the Korean War. By the end of March Ridgeway's hard-driving riflemen were back along the 38th parallel and were ready once again to plunge into North Korea.

All during this period General MacArthur was carrying on a running argument with President Truman and the Joint Chiefs regarding the war strategy in Korea. MacArthur had been shocked by the message that authorized him to evacuate the peninsula and withdraw to Japan. He also flatly disagreed with the restrictions against air strikes north of the Yalu River. He plainly indicated that it was not fair to ask General Ridgeway to fight "a bare-knuckle war with one arm tied behind his back."

MacArthur insisted that China was already in the war as far as it could get, and bombing the Reds' "privileged sanctuary" beyond the Yalu could not possibly do anything except strengthen the U.N. cause. He also favored the use of Chiang Kai-shek's Nationalist Army in fighting on the Chinese mainland. Chiang Kai-shek had been suggesting an invasion from Formosa for some little time. President Truman and the Joint Chiefs opposed this move as one that would, in General Omar Bradley's words, involve the United States "in the wrong war, at the wrong place, at the wrong time, against the wrong enemy." Other member nations of the U.N. also brought strong pressure to bear against the growing risks of full-scale war.

111

On his part, President Truman had not forgotten that MacArthur had told him during their meeting at Wake Island that there was "very little chance" of the Chinese Communists entering the war. He also believed that he had a clearer view than MacArthur of the world picture and felt certain that Russia could very easily be provoked into full-scale fighting that would result in World War III. President Truman also felt that Russia posed a major threat in Europe, and if all of the United States' reserves were committed to Korea, the Soviet Union might strike westward on the European continent.

In the United States, national politics also figured in the controversy. Many Republicans were openly critical of the conduct of what they called "Mr. Truman's War." Some of them even went so far as to accuse the Democratic President of "fighting the war with one eye on the ballot box in next year's election." While this accusation could not be justified if the President's unselfish record in foreign affairs was considered, it was true that the Korean War was unpopular with the American people. They wanted it to be ended. Thus MacArthur's proposal for an all-out drive for a quick victory did receive much public support. On the other hand there were many people who now favored a truce — an end to the war without victory.

The issue between President Truman and General MacArthur was brought to a climax by Republican Congressman Joseph Martin, who wrote to MacArthur asking him what he thought of a speech Martin had made attacking President Truman's war policy. Martin read MacArthur's reply to the House of Representatives on April 5. It read, in part:

"My views and recommendations with respect to the situation created by Red China's entry into war against us in Korea have been submitted to Washington in most complete de-

General MacArthur and Lieutenant General Matthew B. Ridgeway (center) are shown visiting the front shortly after Ridgeway was named commander of the Eighth Army. MacArthur's military secretary, Major General Courtney Whitney, is second from the left. (U.S. Army Photograph)

tail. Generally, these views are well known and generally understood, as they follow the conventional pattern of meeting force with maximum counterforce as we have never failed to do in the past. Your view with respect to the use of the Chinese forces in Formosa is in conflict with neither logic nor this tradition.

"It seems strangely difficult for some to realize that here in Asia is where the Communist conspirators have elected to make their play for global conquest, and that we have joined the issue thus raised on the battlefield; that here we fight Europe's war with arms, while the diplomats there still fight it with words; that if we lose the war to Communism in Asia the fall of Europe is inevitable; win it, and Europe most probably will avoid war and yet preserve freedom. As you point out, we must win. There is no substitute for victory."

General MacArthur's statement was regarded by President Truman as a direct challenge to his authority as Commander in Chief of the nation's Armed Forces. All officers overseas had been instructed to get permission from Washington before making public statements on national policy. This MacArthur had not done. In addition, President Truman said that General MacArthur's words indicated that "he is unable to give his wholehearted support of the United States Government and of the United Nations in matters pertaining to his official duties."

On April 11 President Truman relieved General MacArthur of all of his Far East commands. He was replaced by General Ridgeway. Lieutenant General James A. Van Fleet was named commander of the 8th Army.

Unfortunately, the first word that MacArthur heard of his dismissal came over the radio while he and his wife were entertaining luncheon guests at the American Embassy in Japan. His only comment at this sudden ending to his military career was made to his wife.

"Jeannie," he said gently, "we're going home at last."

General MacArthur returned to the United States in triumph. In city after city he was given a hero's acclaim. New York held one of the biggest parades in its history in his honor. Washington also turned out to welcome one of the nation's greatest military leaders. Late in April he spoke before a joint session of the House of Representatives and the Senate. Many observers felt this was MacArthur's finest hour as an American.

In a totalitarian nation a general in a similar situation probably would have attacked and attempted to overthrow the government. McArthur, however, spoke, he said, "without anger or bitterness." As he had in the past, he freely acknowledged and openly approved the civilian authority over the military in the American system of government. He then outlined what had happened so far in the Korean War and told of his hopes for final victory. His closing words were:

"When I joined the Army half a century ago it was the fulfillment of all my boyish hopes and dreams. The world has turned over many times since I took the oath on the Plain at West Point, and the hopes and dreams have all since vanished. But I still remember the refrain of one of the most popular barracks ballads of that day, which said most proudly that old soldiers never die, they just fade away.

"Like the old soldier of that ballad, I now close my military career and just fade away, an old soldier who tried to do his duty as God gave him the light to see that duty. Good-bye."

President Truman received much bitter criticism for the abrupt way in which he fired General MacArthur. In explaining why he had done so, Truman compared the situation with President Abraham Lincoln's dismissal of

General George B. McClellan, a top commander of the United States Army, in 1862 during the Civil War.

In some ways McClellan and MacArthur were alike. McClellan was called the "Little Napoleon," and MacArthur was sometimes accused of being "as arrogant as a second Napoleon." McClellan, like MacArthur, made public statements criticizing the President's conduct of the war. In fact after one such statement Lincoln said he was reminded of the man whose horse kicked up his hind leg and caught his foot in the stirrup. According to Lincoln, the man said to the horse, "If you're going to get on, I'll get off."

Aside from these small similarities, however, the two cases were quite different. McClellan was relieved from his command for failing to give hot pursuit to the retreating Confederate forces after their defeat in the battle of Antietam. MacArthur, on the other hand, was relieved from his command for wanting to press home the attack against the enemy's supply lifeline more hotly than national policy would allow.

A much more similar case was the dismissal of General Winfield Scott by President James K. Polk at the end of the Mexican War in 1847. Here too national politics played a key role.

General Scott was called "Old Fuss and Feathers" because of his fondness for showy uniforms. He also insisted that his men be paradeground-perfect in their own dress. MacArthur too was a "spit-and-polish" officer who put great stress on dress, his own as well as his men's.

At the start of the Mexican War, General Scott was the commander of the United States Army. As the war progressed, Scott was kept in Washington by President Polk. Many people said that Polk, a Democrat, would not let Scott, a Whig, get into action for fear that he might become a great military hero and thus advance his political party's cause at the expense of Polk and the Democrats.

Scott was finally assigned to an army in the field, and with the defeat of Mexico he became a great hero at home. The Mexicans also respected him because of his firm but kind military rule over them. Scott quickly restored contentment and order to the conquered nation in much the same fashion as MacArthur did later in Japan after World War II. The Mexicans in fact thought so much of Scott that they offered him a million dollars to become their dictator. The general, of course, refused the offer.

While Scott was still in Mexico, several of his officers sent reports criticizing him to President Polk. Scott brought charges against them for insubordination, but Polk restored the officers to duty and ordered Scott home to appear before a board of inquiry.

Like MacArthur, Scott returned home to a thunderous welcome. New York City gave him an ovation. Congress voted him a special gold medal. Robert E. Lee, one of Scott's officers who was later to lead the Confederate Army in the Civil War, said that Scott was "a large man who did a large work and deserved large treatment. Instead," Lee added in words that could have been used later about MacArthur, "he was turned out to pasture like an old horse."

In the Senate the great orator, Daniel Webster, rose up in wrath and declared, also in words that could well describe MacArthur's dismissal, "A man who has performed the most brilliant campaign on military record; a man who has warred against the climate, warred against a thousand unforeseen circumstances, and has carried the flag of his country to the capital of the enemy — honorably, proudly, humanely — to his own permanent honor and the great military credit of his country. And where is he now? Undergoing an inquiry while the high powers he has exercised and executed with so much distinction are transferred to another."

Like MacArthur, General Winfield Scott showed no bitterness or anger. In the end the charges against him were withdrawn, and in 1852 he was the Whig candidate for the Presidency. A century later MacArthur received some Republican support for the Presidential nomination of his party, but he did not get the nomination. Scott was defeated by Franklin Pierce, who had served under Scott in the Mexican War. Thus both old soldiers, Winfield Scott and Douglas MacArthur, faded away.

General MacArthur had said there was "no substitute for victory" in Korea. His superiors felt otherwise. It was now clearly up to them to find some substitute at the conference table, while General Ridgeway and his commanders sought a substitute on the battlefield. The result for long months to come was to be a bloody stalemate.

Eight

Stalemate

Less than a week after General MacArthur spoke before the joint session of Congress, the Chinese Communists launched a major offensive in Korea. Its purpose was to destroy the 8th Army, no matter what the cost in Communist casualties. General James Van Fleet, the new 8th Army commander, was an old hand at beating off sudden enemy onslaughts. He ordered his troops to "roll with the punch," retreating slowly while inflicting as much punishment as possible on the Reds. The punishment inflicted on the enemy was severe.

"Big Jim" Van Fleet was one of the few top-ranking American officers who had earned the right to wear the Combat Infantryman's Badge. He earned that right on the battle-swept beaches of Normandy during the Allied invasion of France in the spring of 1944.

Born in 1892 at Coytesville, New Jersey, "Big Jim" Van Fleet had been graduated from West Point in 1915 along with another promising young officer named Dwight D. Eisenhower. Eisenhower and Van Fleet had played football together at the Military Academy until a knee injury forced "Ike" to give up the sport. "Big Jim" had gone on to become a great fullback on one of the Point's most famous teams.

In World War I Van Fleet had served with the 6th Division in France, and in World War II he returned to France in command of the 4th Division. After the war he was sent to Greece by President Truman to aid that country in its fight against Communist guerrillas. Sending Van Fleet to Greece was in keeping with the historic "Truman Doctrine" of 1947, which stated that it was in the national interest of the United States to prevent any attempt at Soviet domination of the free nations of Europe. Van Fleet's experiences in defeating the Red guerrillas in Greece were to prove valuable in battling the Chinese Reds in Korea.

General Van Fleet had a much more personal stake in the Korean War, however. At this time there were some 140 sons of generals in the United States military service. Of these more than 30 were killed or wounded in Korea. Among these casualties was General Van Fleet's son, the pilot of a B-26. First Lieutenant James Van Fleet, Jr., was killed in action during a night bombing mission while his father was in command of the 8th Army.

When the spring offensive of the Chinese Communists spent itself — at an enormous cost in Red lives — Van Fleet began a counteroffensive. His goal in this drive was, he said, "To find and kill the enemy." This the 8th Army did — in great numbers.

Van Fleet's forces also captured the base of an area

The United Nations delegation, headed by Admiral C. Turner Joy (center), is shown at Kaesong where armistice talks began on July 10, 1951. (U.S. Army Photograph)

The Communist delegation at the first armistice meetings was headed by Chinese Red General Nam II (center). (U.S. Army Photograph)

known as the "Iron Triangle." The Iron Triangle was a vital enemy road center that controlled the land communications network in north central Korea.

The United Nations forces in Korea now seemed to be growing stronger by the day, while the Chinese Communists grew weaker. On Sunday, June 23, at the very moment when the Reds were once again faced with military defeat, Russia's delegate to the United Nations, Jacob Malik, suggested in a radio talk in New York that discussions should begin for a cease-fire in Korea. The Reds had balked at earlier attempts at peace talks, but now they seemed eager to have them begin.

On June 29 General Ridgeway offered to discuss a cease-fire with the top commanders of the Communist forces. After Ridgeway's aides made the arrangements, the talks began on July 10 at Kaesong, a town near the 38th parallel and between the front lines of the opposing armies. Admiral C. Turner Joy, Far East naval commander, was the chief delegate for the United Nations. General Nam Il was in charge of the enemy delegation.

As soon as the truce talks started, the Communist negotiators began to stall. They insisted that the 38th parallel should remain the dividing or demarcation line between the two opposing forces after an armistice was signed. Since the United Nations troops had already driven north of the parallel in many places, Admiral Joy insisted that the truce line be located wherever the battle line was when an armistice was signed. All during the long, hot summer the peace talks dragged on, with the Communists continuing to stall every step of the way.

Meanwhile, not a deadly day passed without casualties along the front. It was as true in Korea as it had been in the days of the Roman legions that a war could only be won by infantry troops seizing and occupying enemy terrain. In this particular war total victory might not now be possible, but even a partial victory required the continued sacrifice of many brave soldiers' lives. Thus, time at the peace table was bought and paid for with the blood of hundreds of heroic yet unsung young riflemen.

In late August the truce talks were broken off by the Communists. Van Fleet's plan had been to keep the military pressure on the Reds but not to engage in any full-scale action that might endanger the peace negotiations. As soon as they were called off, however, Van Fleet launched a series of limited drives aimed at forcing the Reds back to the peace table.

Van Fleet's 8th Army with its ROK and U.N. supporting forces now numbered more than half a million battle-seasoned men. The enemy had some 600,000 men in the field, but the Communists had suffered more than a million casualties since the beginning of the war. Their casualties continued to mount as the 8th Army drove them from several key positions overlooking important sections of the front lines.

Two of these key positions were Bloody and Heartbreak Ridges. They were captured, lost to the enemy and then recaptured several times before they were finally taken and held by the 8th Army. During the seesaw battle for Heartbreak Ridge another American general's son became a casualty. This was Captain William Clark, son of famed World War II General Mark Clark. An infantry officer in the 2nd Division, young Bill Clark in a year of combat was awarded several decorations for heroism, received a battlefield promotion to major and was wounded three times — the third time at Heartbreak Ridge. Young Clark, however, was more fortunate than young Jim Van Fleet. He recovered from his wounds.

By mid-October Van Fleet's tough troops persuaded the

U.S. infantrymen paid dearly to capture Bloody Ridge. (U.S. Army Photograph).

Communists that if they were to meet with any success, it would have to be at the peace table. Truce talks were resumed — this time at the village of Panmunjom — on October 25. And this time the Reds had stopped insisting that the 38th parallel be the post-armistice demarcation line. They continued to find other reasons to stall, however.

By the end of 1951 there was a lull over the battlefield. There were still small, vicious clashes between patrols and sudden, bitter battles between units struggling for key positions. In each of these flaming engagements men were wounded or died, and it made little difference to them whether the battle was described as large or small: it was still war, and the statistics proved it. During the period of the prolonged peace talks the casualty rate was 30,000 a year. But there were no large-scale assaults. General Ridgeway had ordered General Van Fleet to halt all major offensive ground operations.

As both sides went over to the defensive, the action along the main line of resistance (MLR) began to resemble the trench warfare of World War I. Between the two lines of trenches there was a No Man's Land. Hand grenades and trench mortars were as vital as rations. Local attacks and counterattacks often resulted in grim hand-to-hand fighting in which the bayonet and raw courage decided the issue.

Another throwback to earlier warfare was the use of the armored vest by the Korean front-line fighters. Body armor for protection in battle was worn by the warriors of ancient Greece and Rome. Complete suits of chain mail and metal plates were later worn by knights mounted on horseback during the days of chivalry. As gunpowder changed the nature of warfare, armor gradually fell into disuse until it disappeared from the battlefield late in the

17th century. It did not reappear until the middle of the 19th century, and then it was unsuccessful.

During the American Civil War two firms in Connecticut manufactured steel breast plates for Federal troops, but these plates were so heavy that soldiers wearing them had difficulty moving about. In World War I General John J. Pershing, commander of the American Expeditionary Forces, requested that his infantrymen be supplied with body armor made of steel and aluminum. But it too cut down on the mobility of combat troops.

In World War II "flak vests" for aerial gunners were made of lightweight plastics. These were so successful that their use resulted in a 50 per cent reduction in casualties in the 8th Air Force. But it was not until the Korean War that Navy and Marine Corps technicians developed an armored vest that could be worn by infantry combat troops. These vests weighed only eight pounds each and were made of several thicknesses of nylon plates. Although they would not stop a direct hit from a high caliber rifle or machine-gun bullet, they would stop a bayonet thrust, shrapnel and low caliber bullets fired from the Chinese "burp gun," a small automatic weapon. These vests were in wide use by 1952.

During the stalemate the Communists built the most elaborate system of defense fortifications along the front. They were forced to do so because of American air and artillery superiority. Each enemy hill that faced the 8th Army line was actually turned into an underground fortress. A tunnel was dug from the back of the hill into its center. Then the inside of the hill was turned into a honeycomb of passageways. The roof of each passageway was reinforced with logs, and the top of the hill itself acted as further protection. From inside these cave fortresses the Communists then dug additional tunnels with openings facing the battle line. From the mouths of these openings they could fire their artillery guns, pulling them back out of the way when an air attack took place.

The United States troops did not build any such huge underground fortifications along the MLR. In fact they scoffed at one such Red fortress as "Luke the Gook's Castle." American riflemen did make "homes" for themselves at the front, however. This too was similar to World War I, when trench systems were posted with such signs as "Broadway and Forty-Second Street," "State and Madison," and others giving directions and distances to the doughboys' home towns back in America.

In Korea the signs were of a somewhat different nature. They pointed out that you walked through a certain section of a trench "through the courtesy of the 12th Infantry who captured it," or you crossed a bridge on the way to the front "thanks to the 9th Engineers who built it." At one stage of the war the men of the 24th Division planned to erect a sign at Pusan that would read: "You are entering Korea through the courtesy of the 24th Infantry Division." They were not allowed to do so, however.

The food at the front was somewhat similar to the food eaten by the infantrymen in both world wars, although there was a greater variety. Great effort was made to bring hot meals up to the men on the line, but there were many days when the men on the MLR ate mostly C-rations. These included such canned food as different kinds of meat with beans, chicken with noodles, beef stew and hamburgers. There were also certain dry rations such as hard tack, candy bars, powdered coffee, powdered milk and sugar.

While this fare was familiar to most G.I.'s and Marines — particularly those who had fought in World War II — it was a great puzzle to the ROK troops. When they were given their first C-rations, they didn't know what to do with them. The G.I.'s showed them how to open the cans, and the ROK's ate the meat and beans with gusto. The dry rations were a complete mystery to them, however. They finally solved the problem by making sandwiches out of the hard tack, using sugar, powdered milk and powdered coffee as filler.

Life on the MLR was boring but dangerous. With time on their hands the men had little to think about except home and the next patrol they would have to accompany across No Man's Land and into the enemy forward positions. One enlisted man, Sergeant Martin Russ, described his own mood and that of many of the men at the front when he wrote in his diary:

"I hate late afternoon. It always makes me think of New York when the street lights go on and crowds of people leave the office buildings. Late afternoon means it will soon be time for the patrols to get ready to depart. Late afternoon is the time of day when the men are at their lowest."

As night and darkness came down, there was always one light that was clearly visible to the men on the line. This was a searchlight at Panmunjom that was turned on to point out the area to flyers of both sides so they would not bomb it accidentally. The soldiers in the trenches and manning their lonely outposts looked at the light and peered through the surrounding dark toward the enemy, hoping against hope that the peace negotiations would soon come to some final agreement. But the bickering and Communist stalling at the peace table continued — and the routine fighting and dying went on.

To add to the strange, unreal atmosphere at the front, the Communists began broadcasting over loudspeakers to the U.N. troops. These broadcasts across No Man's Land usually consisted of enemy propaganda, including offers

A squad of American infantrymen man a ridge along the MLR. (U.S. Army Photograph)

An American G.I. and a ROK soldier team up at a defense position with Browning automatic rifles. (U.S. Army Photograph)

of kind treatment to any 8th Army men who would surrender. The Reds also played American phonograph records, including a number of Bing Crosby songs. In December Bing Crosby's recording of "White Christmas" was played many times in an effort to make the G.I.'s and Marines homesick enough to quit fighting. When the Chinese were about to attack, rooster, cat and other animal calls were often broadcast over the loudspeakers.

Besides the eventual end of the war, men in combat had two other things to look forward to. These were "R and R," several days of rest and recreation in Japan, and the "Big R," rotation or return to the United States after about a year in action. Almost a million men were flown to Japan on leave and then back to the Korean fighting during the course of the war. Another half-million men were rotated to the United States.

When a man had been in action long enough to be sent home, everybody in his outfit began to take great pains to see that he did not become a casualty before his relief arrived. (All along the roads leading to the front there were frequent signs that read: "Drive carefully! The man you hit may be your relief!") An incident involving Corporal Charles H. Gordon of Liberty, Mississippi, was typical of this attitude of general concern for the safety of a man due for rotation. A squad leader, Gordon was on a night patrol in enemy territory. When the patrol was halfway to its objective, the company radio man caught up with Gordon.

"I've just been talking with the commanding officer," the radio man said. "He says for you to lay down right where you are and don't move. That's a direct order. You're going home tomorrow."

On the home front the Korean War became an important issue in the 1952 national elections. The stalemate at the peace table and along the battle line had made the war more unpopular than ever with the American people.

Early in the year General Dwight D. Eisenhower resigned his post as Supreme Commander of the North Atlantic Treaty Organization (NATO) military forces to campaign for the Republican presidential nomination. (The United States and 11 other nations had signed the North Atlantic Treaty in 1949. Its purpose was to prevent Russian aggression in Europe.) When Eisenhower resigned as NATO commander, General Ridgway replaced him in that job and General Mark Clark was named as the new United Nations commander in Korea.

Soon after Eisenhower was nominated by the Republicans to run for the Presidency, he made a very popular announcement.

"If I am elected," Ike said, "I shall go to Korea."

This personal pledge to try and solve the Korean stalemate was one of the reasons why Eisenhower received some 34 million votes to defeat the Democratic presidential nominee, Adlai Stevenson, in November. This was the greatest number of votes ever given to a candidate for public office in the United States up to this time.

Within a month after he was elected, Ike kept his promise. He made a tour of the Korean battlefront, visiting with several of the top American commanders and trying to seek an honorable solution to the stalemate.

An honorable solution was not easy, however. While Harry Truman was still President, he had struggled equally hard to end the war without sacrificing American principles of individual freedom and justice.

The deadlock in the truce talks was now mainly due to a disagreement over the exchange of prisoners. The United Nations delegates at Panmunjom insisted that prisoners who did not want to return to Communist-controlled North Korea and China should not be forced to do so. The Communists were equally insistent that all cap-

President-elect Dwight D. Eisenhower eats dinner with members of the U.S. Third Division during tour of the Korean battlefront in December 1952. (U.S. Army Photograph)

Ike visits with other U.S. riflemen of the Third Division during his battlefront tour. (U.S. Army Photograph)

tives in the hands of the 8th Army be returned, at gunpoint if necessary. Since it was already known that almost half of the prisoners taken by the 8th Army hated the Communists and feared for their own lives if they were forced to return to the Reds, the United Nations delegates at Panmunjom continued to insist that captives be given a choice in the matter. This was called "voluntary repatriation."

President Truman put the matter clearly when he said, "We are not going to buy peace at the price of returning human beings to slavery or death." When President-elect Eisenhower visited Korea, he was equally firm about this principle. "Forcing these people to return to a life of terror and persecution would be unacceptable to the American code," he said. "It cannot be done."

The deadlock over this issue which began late in 1951 continued through most of 1952. Late in 1952 the truce talks were recessed indefinitely.

On the battlefront, General Clark kept General Ridgeway's earlier orders to General Van Fleet in effect: there were to be no attempts at major assaults. Further, General Clark tried to cut down on the number of casualties caused by the bitter little battles for the endless Korean hills.

A veteran of the grim hill fighting in Italy in World War II, General Clark knew the cost in blood of waging this type of warfare. In describing it, General Clark said:

"Just as in Italy, where we faced the same kind of determined enemy and mountainous terrain, there was always the lure of the next highest hill just ahead of you. The enemy had it for observation which permitted him to hurt your troops. You wanted it so you could look down his throat. But you never really did, for always there was just one more hill, a little higher, up ahead of you. Each hill soaked up men, cost lives."

But despite General Clark's determined effort to avoid costly hill fighting, there were savage battles at "Pork Chop" and "T-Bone" Hills. (They were named for their peculiar shapes.) Fighting here began in late June 1952 and continued for almost a year. Other grim battles were waged for "Old Baldy," "Capitol Hill," "Siberia Hill" and "Bunker Hill."

As the third winter of the Korean War began, the prospects for peace seemed as remote as they had at the beginning of the conflict. The men at the front dug in and waited. The prisoners held by the 8th Army waited — waited and hoped that they would not be forced to return to their former Communist masters. And far to the north, beyond the banks of the Yalu River, another group of prisoners waited — waited and prayed for deliverance from their captivity. These were the thousands of American soldiers and flyers who had been captured by the Communists since the start of the war. There was no doubt in most of these men's minds about wanting to return to the United States. Their only doubt was whether or not they would live to see their homes and loved ones again. These men had experienced and were still experiencing — those who had not already died or been killed by their Communist captors — some of the worst suffering ever endured by any American prisoners of war.

Nine

*Prisoners
of the
Communists*

No one will ever know exactly how many American prisoners of war (POW's) died in Korea. It is known that the prisoner death rate was the highest of any war in United States history. This was mainly due to the barbaric treatment of the POW's by the Communists.

More than 7,000 Americans — most of them Army men — were captured and interned by the North Korean and Chinese Reds. Almost 3,000 of these prisoners died or were killed in captivity. In addition, several thousand service men were killed as soon as they were captured. The Army alone lost more than 1,000 men in such front-line atrocities. The fate of several hundred other men who were known to have been prisoners of the Communists was never disclosed by the Chinese despite stern demands from the United States government.

After they were captured, many Americans were brutally herded toward Communist prison camps. These movements away from the front lines often turned into death marches on which the weak and wounded were shot or left to die. When they arrived at the POW camps, the men found the bodies of many earlier prisoners. In some cases these bodies were stacked like cord wood outside the mud huts that served as barracks. Those who were still alive were slowly starving from the inadequate diet of cracked corn, millet and an occasional meal of rice. The POW's were so desperate for food that many of them ate grass, worms and grasshoppers. In one camp alone between 1,600 and 1,800 men died from starvation and disease during the course of the war.

After the men had been prisoners for several months, their captors tried to convert them to Communism. The POW's were given more and better food, and then daily classes were held in the Communist way of life. These "classes" usually consisted of endless lectures on what was wrong with the United States and what was right about Communist countries. Prisoners who gave any sign of agreeing with such indoctrination were praised as "peace fighters" and "progressives" by the Chinese. Those men who resisted the Reds were denounced as "reactionaries" by the Communists. One such bitter foe of the Reds was Army Sergeant Lloyd W. Pate.

Sergeant Pate was only 18 when he was captured. He was a prisoner for two and a half years. He fought his cruel captors tooth-and-nail all during his imprisonment.

"I didn't like a guy to stand over me and preach things I knew were a pack of lies," Pate said. "I'm an American and I'm proud of it. I didn't like any Red to try and tell me my government and my people were no good when I knew they were a thousand times better than his. They said Americans were starving to death in the States and that we started the war — both lies. I felt it was my duty to cause those Red jerks as much trouble as possible."

Pate was one of a group of men who gave the Communists a hard time from the moment they were captured. The men were moved toward POW camps at night. These marches were made along narrow mountain roads. When it grew dark, Pate and his G.I. buddies would move up close to one of their guards and shove him over a cliff. They got rid of some 20 Red guards in this fashion.

The Reds carried their food in long sock-like pouches tied to their belts. Pate and his friends also managed from time to time to slit these pouches so the food would spill out as the guards walked along.

Some captured G.I.'s were forced to drive Communist trucks carrying supplies. There was a Red guard in each truck, and if the guard fell asleep the G.I. would leap from the cab and let the truck and the guard hurtle over a cliff.

Once they reached the POW camp, the hard core of resistance men continued their silent war with their captors. Not only did they stubbornly refuse to accept any of the Communist propaganda they were taught in the indoctrination classes, but they also tried to prevent any of their fellow prisoners from being sympathetic with Red teachings. Some American POW's were tempted to collaborate with their captors in the hope of getting better treatment. Pate and his fellow reactionaries threatened these collaborators with physical punishment. In some cases they actually carried out these threats.

"We usually didn't have to beat up a guy more than once before he got the word," Pate said.

Pate did not get off easily for his resistance to the Communists. On one occasion he was put into solitary confinement for more than a month. No sunlight was allowed to enter his cell, and Pate was forced to sit 18 hours a day cross-legged on the floor. When he was released, Pate's hair had turned gray.

On another occasion Pate's hands were handcuffed behind his back for a week, and he was made to stare at the glaring sun for as long as half an hour at a time. Once he almost died after being placed naked in a hole in the ground with the temperature at 30 degrees below zero. He still refused to collaborate with his captors, because he knew that if he once agreed to even their smallest request there would be no turning back.

During his long months of captivity Pate thoroughly learned the Communist techniques for converting men to their cause. In describing this technique Pate said: "First, there is a starvation period of up to six months. This kills off the weak and wounded. Then there are short lectures on Communism. Gradually the Reds spot the ones who are falling for their line. They take them aside and give them special lectures on the theories of Marx, Engels, Lenin, and Stalin. Then they dream up some plan and try to push it through. In Korea it was germ warfare. They get the men to sign petitions, make voice recordings, and write articles. They try to get the men to do something no matter how small. Then they hold this over the POW's heads, telling them they're going to get punished anyway when they get home. Once a man does anything for them, they've got him hooked."

Sergeant Pate's germ warfare reference was to an elaborate propaganda campaign attempted by the Communists. The Reds claimed that the United Nations forces were engaging in germ warfare in Korea, and even succeeded in forcing some American prisoners of war to sign statements that this was true. The claims were never proven and in time were generally recognized as a hoax.

After the war Sergeant Pate was awarded a special Army commendation ribbon for his resistance efforts as a prisoner of war in Korea. In describing the lessons he had learned from his experiences, Sergeant Pate pointed out that in the Communist indoctrination classes the Red instructors in history, and particularly American history, were much better educated in the facts than the average soldier, and it was possible for the Reds to twist the facts around to meet their own needs.

"It is right at this point," Sergeant Pate said, "that we can stop them. If our soldiers are taught American history and politics and about how the economic system works in the United States, they will be able to argue against the lies the Communists tell. The Army can do some of this, but not all. It's mostly up to the soldier's parents and his school and his church before he gets into the Army."

Another prisoner who firmly refused to become a Communist collaborator despite harsh treatment and threats of torture was General William Dean. Dean was never thrown into a POW camp but was held in isolation in various places in North Korea. His Communist captors constantly tried to get him to sign "confessions" that he was a war criminal and that the Americans had committed numerous atrocities. They also tried to get him to broadcast over the radio and admit that General MacArthur had ordered Syngman Rhee to start the war.

Early in his period of captivity, Dean was forced to sit cross-legged for days at a time. At one point he was forced to strip to his shorts in an unheated room with the temperature below freezing. He was questioned by relays of interrogators for periods of 44 and 68 hours without letup. During World War II Dean had gone as long as four days without sleep, so he did not regard his Korean experience as being especially difficult. He was, however, suffering from stomach and kidney trouble and malaria and was afraid that in his weakened condition he might tell his captors some details about defense plans with which he was familiar.

When he was threatened with torture — forcing water under high pressure into his mouth — he said, "That sounds fine to me. The shape I'm in that should kill me off quickly." The Reds also threatened to drive bamboo splinters under his finger nails. Dean decided that if he actually was about to be tortured he would make a break for it and get shot to prevent himself from giving any information that might be of help to the enemy.

At one point he did manage to get hold of a Chinese "burp gun", but the gun jammed and before he could use it on his guards he was overpowered.

After some months the Reds stopped questioning their prize prisoner for fear they might kill him. Living in isolation, General Dean's greatest problem became passing time. He was afraid he might lose his mind if he failed to find some way to occupy himself, so he began working arithmetic problems in his head. One day while he was doing some of these mental problems, one of his guards saw Dean's lips moving and ordered him to quit counting to himself unless given permission to do so.

Dean also passed the time by catching flies. He kept an accurate count of the flies he killed during his captivity. The total came to 40,671. He figured his daily efforts and results like a ball player figuring his batting average. At one time he was batting as high as .760 in the "fly league."

No one in the United States knew that General Dean had been taken prisoner until almost a year and a half after his capture. On December 19, 1951, his name appeared on a prisoner of war list issued by the Communists. A short time later, a news report by a Communist correspondent, Wilfred Burchett, who interviewed Dean in North Korea, was published in newspapers around the world. On January 2, 1952, Dean learned that his family knew he was alive. He had telegrams from his wife, mother and daughter. His daughter told him he had a grandson born March 24, 1951.

Toward the end of his captivity when it appeared that there was finally to be some sort of peace settlement at Panmunjom, the Communists tried another technique on General Dean. They tried to get him to join their army! Dean laughed at the offer.

General Dean, like Sergeant Pate, learned a number of lessons from his experiences as a prisoner of the Communists. He was released from captivity at Panmunjom on September 4, 1953, and returned to the United States to a hero's welcome. Dean insisted he was no hero — "just a dog-faced soldier." He added: "We must present a factual world better than the Communist dream. We must have political answers simple enough for the dullest to understand. We must, each of us, know and understand the things for which we fight. An army can be a show window for democracy only if every man in it is convinced that it does fight for a free world, for the kind of government he wants himself."

Early in 1953 there was very little fighting along the front. On February 11, Lieutenant General Maxwell D. Taylor, another paratrooper veteran of World War II, replaced General Van Fleet as the commander of the 8th Army. Van Fleet returned to the United States for retirement.

The enemy attacks increased later in the spring, but

they were successfully beaten off by the United States 25th Division and several ROK divisions. Again the Chinese suffered heavy casualties.

In February General Clark had suggested that both sides exchange their sick and wounded prisoners. This exchange — known as Operation "Little Switch" — began in late April. About 700 United Nations prisoners were exchanged for more than 6,000 Communists.

Armistice negotiations were also resumed in April. The Communists were still balking over "voluntary repatriation." Some 60,000 of the more than 130,000 North Koreans and Chinese held by the United Nations forces continued to say that they did not want to return to their homelands. This was a severe blow to the Communists, who could not permit the loss of face that would result from such mass desertions. The question was apparently settled by allowing teams of officials from both sides to interview prisoners and attempt to persuade those who were reluctant to be repatriated to change their minds. But just when it seemed the war was about to end, the peace negotiations were violently interrupted by Syngman Rhee.

Old patriot Rhee had never agreed to a permanent division of the land which he had been fighting all of his life to unite. As the peace talks at Panmunjom neared their conclusion, Rhee warned General Mark Clark and others that he would not sign any truce that included such a division. When it became clear that a truce was about to be signed with or without his agreement, Rhee took matters into his own hands.

On the night of June 17 under Rhee's orders ROK guards in South Korean prison camps opened the gates and freed many of the North Korean prisoners who did not want to be repatriated. Some 27,000 anti-Communist prisoners were thus allowed to escape.

Lieutenant General Maxwell D. Taylor (left) was the U.S. Eighth Army commander, and General Mark Clark (right) was Commander in Chief of the U.N. Command in the final months of the war. They are shown at the front with an officer of the Greek battalion which was attached to the U.S. Third Infantry Division. (U.S. Army Photograph)

The Chinese Communists were, of course, furious. Rhee's action was also criticized by the heads of the United Nations, who said it threatened the proposed armistice. This was true. A few days later the Reds broke off the peace talks and demanded that all of their men who were prisoners, including those Rhee had released, be returned to them. General Clark pointed out that it would be impossible to round up the thousands of men who had been released because they had now disappeared into the civilian population.

Great pressure was now brought on Syngman Rhee both by General Clark and President Eisenhower. Rhee was told bluntly that unless he did agree to the terms of the armistice he would get no further military support from the United States. If he did agree to the terms, he was promised both continued military and economic aid after the war. Rhee finally bowed to the inevitable.

General Clark's efforts to get the Chinese to resume the peace talks were also successful. They got under way once more early in July. The armistice was signed on July 27, 1953, at Panmunjon. Chinese Premier Kim Sung said he would not attend the ceremonies unless reporters and all anti-Communists were barred. Clark refused to agree to this demand, so he and the Chinese premier were not present. Lieutenant General William Harrison led the United Nations signers, and Lieutenant General Nam Il was in charge of the Communist delegation.

That night at 10 P.M. the guns along the front fell silent. The Korean War was over — or at least the shooting had stopped. No peace treaty was signed; nor would one be signed within the foreseeable future. Both sides maintained their armies on either side of the military demarcation line, a line which the United States 8th Army and other United Nations forces still guard today.

When the guns stopped firing on the night of July 27, there was very little rejoicing among the G.I.'s, Leathernecks, ROK's and other U.N. forces. An indecisive war had come to an indecisive conclusion, and all any of the men along the main line of resistance wanted was to get home just as soon as possible.

Operation "Big Switch" — the final exchange of prisoners — began in August and ended in September. More than 70,000 North Koreans and about 6,000 Chinese finally agreed to be repatriated. The Reds released about 3,500 Americans, some 1,300 other U.N. troops, and about 8,000 South Koreans. At one time the Communists had claimed they had captured almost 70,000 South Koreans. The pitifully few ROK's they actually returned was further evidence of the barbaric treatment of prisoners of war by the Communists.

Freedom Village was the name of the camp near Panmunjom where the United Nations troops were received. It was here that such valiant American POW's as Sergeant Pate and General Dean returned once again to the free world they had risked their lives to preserve. And it was also here that ugly stories began to be told by some of the returning POW's about how a few of their fellow Americans had collaborated with the Communists during their captivity.

For many months there had been rumors of such collaboration. The fact that some men had signed the germ warfare "confessions" had surprised many people in the United States. This was explained with reports of the tremendous pressures used against the prisoners by the Reds. But other Americans had also signed Red "peace petitions" and made radio propaganda broadcasts. These too were explained away by saying the Communists got Americans to do these things by using "brainwashing" methods.

145

During Operation "Little Switch" it was rumored that a few Americans among those exchanged seemed somewhat sympathetic toward the Communist cause. They gave no evidence of having been "brainwashed," however. Sergeant Pate's explanation of the Red techniques in winning converts perhaps explained why even a few men were tempted to believe the Communist teachings.

Not so easily explained was the fact that 21 American prisoners of war, when given their choice of returning to America or remaining in Red China, refused to return to their homeland. While this was a small number compared with the thousands of Reds who had refused to be repatriated, it was hard for Americans to believe that any United States soldier could desert his native land.*

For several years after the war the stories about American collaboration with the Chinese Reds were told and retold until they were exaggerated beyond all truth. The inhuman treatment the POW's had received was ignored, and the stories of the few men who had collaborated were over-emphasized. The matter became such a concern to United States government officials that the following Code of Conduct was drawn up for all American servicemen; it was signed by President Eisenhower in 1955:

THE MILITARY CODE OF CONDUCT

I. I am an American fighting man. I serve in the forces which guard my country and our way of life. I am prepared to give my life in their defense.

---

* By 1964, more than a decade after the signing of the armistice in Korea, only five of the 21 turncoats were still in China. One had died there. Another had married a Czechoslovakian girl he met in China and moved with her to Czechoslovakia. A third had married a Polish girl and moved to Poland. A fourth U.S. Army defector left China bound for Belgium, his birthplace. Twelve others had returned to the United States.

II.   I will never surrender of my own free will. If in command I will never surrender my men while they still have the means to resist.

III.   If I am captured I will continue to resist by all means available. I will make every effort to escape and aid others to escape. I will accept neither parole nor special favors from the enemy.

IV.   If I become a prisoner of war, I will keep faith with my fellow prisoners. I will give no information or take part in any action which might be harmful to my comrades. If I am senior, I will take command. If not, I will obey the lawful orders of those appointed over me and will back them up in every way.

V.   When questioned, should I become a prisoner of war, I am bound to give only my name, rank, service number, and date of birth. I will evade answering further questions to the utmost of my ability. I will make no oral or written statements disloyal to my country and its allies or harmful to their cause.

VI.   I will never forget that I am an American fighting man, responsible for my actions, and dedicated to the principles which made my country free. I will trust in my God and in the United States of America.

Today a clearer picture has emerged of the conduct of American POW's in Korea. It is evident that United States servicemen who became prisoners of the North Korean and Chinese Reds actually behaved as well as or better than American prisoners had behaved in all of the nation's other wars. The fact that the last two years of the Korean War were fought along a 10-mile-wide strip of land with neither side able to win a military victory colored many Americans' thoughts. They were sick of the conflict and somewhat ashamed of not having won it. They vented some of their feelings of guilt on innocent targets: the American POW's.

Always fascinated by "firsts," many Americans also said the Korean War was the first conflict that the United States had failed to win. This too was untrue. The War of 1812 ended equally indecisively. And further, in a major sense the Korean War *was* a victory, a victory over Communist aggression.

Actually Americans had no cause to be ashamed of either their own men in Korea or the outcome of the fighting. For it was here, for the first time in history, that America joined with the other free nations of the West and fought the Communists to a standstill. America could be proud of its key role in the first United Nations war, as it can be proud today of the role it plays in defending South Korea along the military demarcation line which the 8th Army aptly calls "Freedom's Frontier."

As for the men who fought in Korea, Secretary of the Army Cyrus R. Vance said on March 15, 1963:

"No braver war was ever fought, under more trying conditions, than that which was fought in Korea. In the Army, for example, 41,835 awards for valor, 117,315 Purple Hearts attest to this. The men were magnificent, and we should remember them so."

Medal of Honor Awards for the Korean War

"The men were magnificent, and we should remember them so."
— Secretary of the Army Cyrus R. Vance

Medals of Honor were awarded to 131 members of the United States Armed Forces for their heroic exploits during the Korean War. This was a greater number of Medal of Honor winners than there were in World War I, which many Americans have long thought of as a more heroic conflict than that in Korea. Some 123 men won the nation's highest award for valor in World War I, and 430 heroes earned it in World War II.

Army men were awarded 78 Medals of Honor for the Korean War, members of the Marine Corps earned 42, Navy men seven, and Air Force flyers four. Only 39 of these 131 men lived to receive their awards. Several officers and men were promoted in addition to being awarded the Medal of Honor.

Listed below, by branch of military service, are the men who earned the Medal of Honor in the Korean War:

ARMY

Adams, Stanley T., M/Sgt.	24th Inf. Div.	Olathe, Kans.
*Barker, Charles H.	7th Inf. Div.	Pickens, S. C.
*Bennett, Emory L., Pfc.	3rd Inf. Div.	Cocoa, Fla.
Bleak, David B., Sgt.	40th Inf. Div.	Shelley, Idaho
*Brittin, Nelson V., Sfc.	24th Inf. Div.	Audubon, N.J.
Brown, Melvin L., Pfc.	1st Cav. Div.	Mahaffey, Pa.
Burke, Lloyd L., 1st Lt.	1st Cav. Div.	Stuttgart, Ark.
*Burris, Tony K., Sfc.	2nd Inf. Div.	Blanchard, Okla.
*Charlton, Cornelius H., Sgt.	25th Inf. Div.	New York, N.Y.
*Collier, Gilbert G.	40th Inf. Div.	Tichnor, Ark.

*Collier, John W., Cpl.	25th Inf. Div.	Worthington, Ky.
*Coursen, Samuel S., 1st Lt.	1st Cav. Div.	Madison, N.J.
*Craig, Gordon M., Cpl.	1st Cav. Div.	E. Bridgewater, Mass
Crump, Jerry K., Cpl.	3rd Inf. Div.	Forest City, N. C.
Dean, William F., Maj. Gen.	24th Inf. Div.	Berkeley, Calif.
*Desiderio, Reginald, Capt.	25th Inf. Div.	Gilroy, Calif.
*Dodd, Carl H., 1st Lt.	24th Inf. Div.	Kenvir, Ky.
*Duke, Ray E., Sfc.	24th Inf. Div.	Whitwell, Tenn.
*Edwards, Junior D., Sfc.	2nd Inf. Div.	Indianola, Iowa
*Essebagger, John Jr., Cpl.	3rd Inf. Div.	Holland, Mich.
*Faith, Don C. Jr., Lt. Col.	7th Inf. Div.	Washington, Ind.
*George, Charles, Pfc.	45th Inf. Div.	Whittier, N.C.
*Gilliland, Charles L., Cpl.	3rd Inf. Div.	Yellville, Ark.
*Goodblood, Clair, Cpl.	3rd Inf. Div.	Burnham, Me.
*Hammond, Lester Jr., Cpl.	187th Regtl.	Quincy, Ill.
*Handrich, Melvin O., M/Sgt.	25th Inf. Div.	Manawa, Wis.
*Hanson, Jack G., Pfc.	7th Inf. Div.	Galveston, Tex.
*Hartell, Lee R., 1st Lt.	2nd Inf. Div.	Danbury, Conn.
Harvey, Raymond, Capt.	7th Inf. Div.	Pasadena, Calif.
Henry, Frederick F., 1st Lt.	2nd Inf. Div.	Clinton, Okla.
Hernandez, Rodolfo P., Cpl.	187th Regtl.	Fowler, Calif.
Ingman, Einar H., Sgt.	7th Inf. Div.	Tomahawk, Wis.
*Jecelin, William R., Sgt.	25th Inf. Div.	Baltimore, Md.
*Jordan, Mack A., Pfc.	24th Inf. Div.	Collins, Miss.
*Kanell, Billie G.	25th Inf. Div.	Poplar Bluff, Mo.
*Kaufman, Loren R., Sfc.	2nd Inf. Div.	The Dalles, Ore.
*Knight, Noah O., Pfc.	3rd Inf. Div.	Jefferson, S.C.
Kouma, Ernest R., M/Sgt.	2nd Inf. Div.	Dwight, Neb.
*Krysyzowski, Edward C., Capt.	2nd Inf. Div.	Cicero, Ill.
*Kyle, Darwin K., 2nd Lt.	3rd Inf. Div.	Racine, W. Va.
Lee, Hubert L., M/Sgt.	2nd Inf. Div.	Leland, Miss.
*Libby, George D., Sgt.	24th Inf. Div.	Waterbury, Conn.
*Long, Charles R., Sgt.	2nd Inf. Div.	Kansas City, Mo.
*Lyell, William F., Cpl.	7th Inf. Div.	Old Hickory, Tenn.
*Martinez, Benito, Cpl.	25th Inf. Div.	Fort Hancock, Tex.
*McGovern, Robert M., 1st Lt.	1st Cav. Div.	Washington, D.C.
*Mendonca, LeRoy A., Sgt.	3rd Inf. Div.	Honolulu, Hawaii
Millett, Lewis L., Capt.	25th Inf. Div.	Mechanic Falls, Me
Miyamura, Hiroshi H., Cpl.	3rd Inf. Div.	Gallup, N.M.
Mize, Ola L., M/Sgt.	3rd Inf. Div.	Gadsden, Ala.
*Moyer, Donald R., Sfc.	25th Inf. Div.	Oakland, Mich.
*Ouellette, Joseph R., Pfc.	2nd Inf. Div.	Lowell, Mass.
*Page, John U.D., Lt. Col.	10th Corps Artillery	St. Paul, Minn.
*Pendleton, Charles F., Cpl.	3rd Inf. Div.	Fort Worth, Tex.

*Pililaau, Herbert K., Pfc.	2nd Inf. Div.	Waianae, Oahu, Hawaii
Pittman, John A., Sgt.	2nd Inf. Div.	Tallula, Miss.
*Pomeroy, Ralph E., Pfc.	7th Inf. Div.	Quinwood, W. Va.
*Porter, Donn. F., Sgt.	25th Inf. Div.	Baltimore, Md.
*Red Cloud, Mitchell Jr., Cpl.	24th Inf. Div.	Merrillan, Wis.
Rodriguez, Joseph C., Sgt.	7th Inf. Div.	San Bernardino, Calif.
Rosser, Ronald E., Cpl.	2nd Inf. Div.	Crooksville, Ohio
*Schoonover, Dan D., Cpl.	7th Inf. Div.	Boise, Idaho
Schowalter, Edward R. Jr., 1st Lt.	7th Inf. Div.	Metairie, La.
*Shea, Richard T. Jr., 1st Lt.	7th Inf. Div.	Portsmouth, Va.
*Sitman, William S., Sfc.	2nd Inf. Div.	Bellwood, Pa.
*Smith, David M., Pfc.	2nd Inf. Div.	Livingston, Ky.
*Speicher, Clifton T., Cpl.	40th Inf. Div.	Gray, Pa.
Stone, James L., 1st Lt.	1st Cav. Div.	Pine Bluff, Ark.
Story, Luther H., Pfc.	2nd Inf. Div.	Buena Vista, Ga.
*Sudut, Jerome A., 2nd Lt.	25th Inf. Div.	Wausau, Wis.
*Thompson, William, Pfc.	25th Inf. Div.	New York, N.Y.
*Turner, Charles W., Sfc.	2nd Inf. Div.	Boston, Mass.
*Watkins, Travis E., M/Sgt.	2nd Inf. Div.	Overton, Tex.
West, Ernest E., Pfc.	25th Inf. Div.	Wurtland, Ky.
Wilson, Benjamin F., 1st Lt.	7th Inf. Div.	Vashon, Wash.
*Wilson, Richard G., Pfc.	11th Airborne Div.	Cape Girardeau, Mo.
*Womack, Bryant H., Pfc.	25th Inf. Div.	Mills Springs, N.C.
*Young, Robert H., Pfc.	1st Cav. Div.	Vallejo, Calif.

NAVY

*Benfold, Edward C., Hospital Corpsman	1st Marine Div.	Camden, N.J.
Charette, William R., Hospital Corpsman	1st Marine Div.	Ludington, Mich.
*DeWert, Richard D., Hospitalman	1st Marine Div.	Taunton, Mass.
*Hammond, Francis C., Hospitalman	1st Marine Div.	Alexandria, Va.
Hudner, Thomas J.Jr., Lt. JG	32nd Fighter Sqdn.	Fall River, Mass.
*Kilmer, John E., Hospitalman	2nd Helicopter Sqdn.	Los Angeles, Calif.
*Koelsch, John K., Lt. JG	1st Marine Div.	Houston, Tex.

MARINE CORPS

*Abrell, Charles G., Cpl.	1st Marine Div.	Terre Haute, Ind.
Barber, William E., Capt.	1st Marine Div.	West Liberty, Ky.
*Baugh, William B., Pfc.	1st Marine Div.	Harrison, Ohio
Cafferata, Hector A. Jr., Pfc.	1st Marine Div.	Boonton, N.J.
*Champagne, David B., Cpl.	1st Marine Div.	Wakefield, R. I.
*Christianson, Stanley, Pfc.	1st Marine Div.	Mindoro, Wis.
Commisskey, Henry A., Capt.	1st Marine Div.	Hattiesburg, Miss.

Books
About
the Korean
War

The Army Almanac (Stackpole Company, 1959).

Biderman, Albert D., *March to Calumny: The Story of American POW's in the Korean War* (Macmillan, 1963).

Clark, Mark W., *From the Danube to the Yalu* (Harper, 1954).

Dean, William F., *General Dean's Story* (Viking, 1954).

Donovan, Frank R., *The Medal: The Story of the Medal of Honor* (Dodd, Mead, 1962).

Dupuy, R. Ernest, *The Compact History of the United States Army* (Hawthorn Books, 1956).

Fehrenbach, T. R., *This Kind of War: A Study in Unpreparedness* (Macmillan, 1963).

Greer, Andrew C., *The New Breed: The Story of the U.S. Marines in Korea* (Harper, 1952).

Goldberg, Alfred, ed., *A History of the United States Air Force, 1907-1957* (Van Nostrand, 1958).

Gurney, Gene, *Five Down and Glory: A History of the American Air Ace* (Putnam, 1958).

Karig, Walter and others, *Battle Report: The War in Korea* (Holt, 1952).

Kinkead, Eugene, *In Every War But One* (Norton, 1959).

Leckie, Robert, *Conflict: The History of the Korean War, 1950-53 (Putnam,* 1962).

Leckie, Robert, *March to Glory* (World, 1960).

Marshall, S. L. A., *Pork Chop Hill: The American Fighting Man in Action, Korea, Spring, 1953* (Morrow, 1956).

Pate, Lloyd W., *Reactionary!* (Harper, 1956).

Peffer, Nathaniel, *The Far East* (University of Michigan Press, 1958).

Potter, Elmer B. and Fredland, J. R., eds., *The United States and World Sea Power* (Prentice-Hall, 1955).

Russ, Martin, *The Last Parallel: A Marine's War Journal* (Holt, 1957).

Schott, Joseph L., *Above and Beyond: The Story of the Congressional Medal of Honor* (Putnam, 1963).

U.S. Marine Corps., *U.S. Marine Operations in Korea,* 4 vols. (Government Printing Office, 1954-62).

U.S. Office of the Chief of Military History, *Korea: 1950* (Government Printing Office, 1952).

U.S. Office of the Chief of Military History, *Korea: 1951-53* (Government Printing Office, 1956).

U.S. Office of the Chief of Military History, *Military Advisors in Korea: KMAG in Peace and War* (Government Printing Office, 1962).

Whitney, Courtney, *MacArthur: His Rendezvous With History* (Knopf 1956).

Index

Aces. *See* Heroes and Aces
Airplanes
  Russian built, 81, 83-4
  United States, 53-6
Almond, Edward, 86, 88
  Frozen Chosen, battle, 90-105
Armored vest, 126
Atlantic Charter, 35-6
Atrocities, 60, 135-41

Badoeng Strait, 58
Barber, William E., 92, 94, 95-6, 98-9
Battles, campaigns, attacks, etc.
  Bloody Ridge, 123
  Bunker Hill, 134
  Capitol Hill, 134
  Frozen Chosen, 88-105
  Heartbreak Ridge, 123
  Inchon landing, 62-3
  No-Name Ridge, 59

  Old Baldy, 134
  Pork Chop Hill, 134
  Pusan beachhead, 44-6, 51-61
  Siberia Hill, 134
  T-Bone Hill, 134
"Bloody Ridge" (battle), 123
Bradley, Omar, 78
Brainwashing, 138, 145-6
"Bunker Hill" (battle), 134

Cafferata, Hector, 94-6
Cairo, Egypt
  Allied leaders meet, 34
"Can Do" outfit, 42
"Capitol Hill" (battle), 134
Casualties, 41-2
  China, 96, 105, 123
  Great Britain, 42
  North Korea, 59
  South Korea, 41; of prisoners, 145
  Turkey, 42

155

United Nations, 41-2
United States, 41-2, 81, 96, 105;
  of prisoners, 135-6
Chiang Kai-shek, 80
China
  background of Korean conflict,
    31-2, 34
  branded "aggressor" by U.N.,
    110-11
  casualties, 96, 105, 123
  combat forces in North Korea, 79-
    81
Chinhung-ni, North Korea, 90, 92,
  99
Clark, Eugene F., 68-9
Clark, Mark, 133-4
  named U.N. Commander in Ko-
    rea, 131
  Operation "Little Switch", 142
Clark, William, 123
Collins, J. Lawton, 63, 67, 68
Congressional Medal of Honor, 75,
  84
  list of winners, 149-52
  Barber, William E., 96
  Cafferata, Hector, 96
  Davis, George A., Jr., 84
  Dean, William, 30
  Lopez, Baldomero, 74-5
  Loring, Charles J., Jr., 84
  Luke, Frank, 84
  MacArthur, Douglas, 64
  Page, John, 101
  Sebille, Louis J., 84
  Walmsley, John S., Jr., 84
Craig, Edward, 57

Davis, George A., Jr., 84
Davis, Raymond, 98-9
Dean, June, 20, 141
Dean, Mildred, 20, 23, 29-30
Dean, William, 19-30
  military governor of South Korea,
    36-7
  prisoner of the Communists,
    139-41
Dean, William, Jr., 20

"Dog faces", 86

Eisenhower, Dwight D.
  elected president, 131
  General MacArthur and, 65
  General Van Fleet and, 120
  resigns NATO command, 131

"Flying Fish Channel", 63, 71
Food, 127-8
"Freedom's Frontier", 148
Frozen Chosen (battle), 88-105

Germ warfare, 138
Great Britain
  casualties, 42
  combat forces, 41, 57, 70

Hagaru-ri, North Korea, 90, 92
Halsey, William F,
  quoted, 76
Hamhung, North Korea, 90
"Heartbreak Ridge" (battle), 123
Hermit Kingdom, 32
Heroes and Aces
  Barber, William, E., 92, 94, 95-6,
    98-9
  Cafferata, Hector, 94-6
  Davis, George A., Jr., 84
  Lopez, Baldomero, 74-5
  Loring, Charles J., Jr., 84
  Page, John, 100-3
  Pate, Lloyd W., 136-9
  Sebille, Louis J., 84
  Walmsley, John S., Jr., 84
Hiroshima, Japan
  atomic bomb, 34
Han Doo Kyoo, 29
Hope, Bob, 87
Hudson, William G., 54
"Human Sea" attacks, 53, 60
Hungnam, North Korea, 92

Inchon, South Korea, 63
  evacuated, 110
  landing, 62-3, 67-76
Independence (newspaper), 33
"Iron Triangle", 122

Japan
  background of Korean conflict,
    31-4
Joy, C. Turner, 122

Kaesong, South Korea
  truce talks, 122
Kean, William, 58
  quoted, 60
Kieffer, Charles F., 101
Kim II Sung, 144
Kimpo Airfield, 75-6
Korea. *See* North Korea; South
  Korea
Korea (peninsula)
  history, 31-2
  map, 18
  size, 31
Korean War
  books about, 153-4
  chronology, 11-14
  map, 18
Koto-ri, North Korea, 90, 92, 99-100
  airstrip, 101

League of Nations, 35
Lie, Trygve, 37
Little, James W., 54
"Long March", 80
Lopez, Baldomero, 74-5
Loring, Charles J., Jr., 84
"Luke the Gook's Castle," 127

MacArthur, Arthur, 65
MacArthur, Douglas, 64-7
  General Ridgeway and, 106-7
  General Walker and, 60-1, 86
  Inchon plan, 61-3, 67-9
  Inchon landing, 69-76
  President Truman and, 39, 79
  relieved of his command, 111-18
  speaks against atrocities, 60
  Yalu River drive, plan, 90
MacArthur, Jean, 65
McClellan, George B.
  dismissal compared with General
    MacArthur's, 116
Malik, Jacob, 122

Mao Tse-tung
  quoted, 78
Map, Korean Theater of War, 18
Martin, Joseph, 112
Masan, South Korea, 58
Medal of Honor. *See* Congressional
  Medal of Honor
Military Code of Conduct, 146-7
Military Leaders. *See* index entries
  on following:
  Almond, Edward
  Collins, J. Lawton
  Craig, Edward
  Dean, William
  Joy, C. Turner
  Kean, William
  MacArthur, Douglas
  Partridge, Earl E.
  Puller, Lewis B.
  Ridgeway, Matthew B.
  Shepherd, Lemuel C.
  Sherman, Forrest
  Smith, Oliver
  Stratemeyer, George E.
  Struble, Arthur
  Van Fleet, James A.
  Walker, Walton
  Williams, Sam
Mines
  Wonsan habor, 87
Miryang, South Korea, 58-9
Missouri, 66, 70-1
Mitchell, William, 65

Naktong Bulge, 58-9
Nagasaki, Japan
  atomic bomb, 34
Nam II, 122
"No-Name" Ridge," 59
North Korea
  army, 24, 52-3
  casualties, 59
  map, 18
  People's Democratic Republic es-
    tablished, 36

"Old Baldy" (battle), 134
Operation "Big Switch", 145

Operation "Little Switch", 142
Operation "Yo-Yo", 87

Page, John, 100-3
Palmi-do (island), 69, 71
Panmunjom
  truce talks, 125, 128, 131
Partridge, Earl E., 53
Pate, Lloyd W., 136-9
Patton, George, 46, 48-9, 51
People's Democratic Republic. *See*
  North Korea
"Pork Chop Hill" (battle), 134
Potsdam, Germany
  Allied conference, 34
Prisoners
  exchanges of, 142, 145
  freed by Syngman Rhee, 142-3
  North Koreans, 77
  of the Communists, 134-41
  South Koreans, 145
  United States, 145
  voluntary repatriation, 131, 133,
    134, 142, 145
Propaganda, 128-9, 138-9
Puller, Lewis B., 72, 74, 99-100
Purple Heart awards, 148
Pusan beachhead, 44-6, 51-61
Pyongyang, North Korea
  capital, 36

Republic of Korea. *See* South Korea
Rhee, Syngman, 30-4
  elected president of South Korea,
    23, 36
  frees prisoners, 142-3
  government returned to, 76
  ROK military forces placed under
    MacArthur, 39
  Russia propagandizes, 37
Ridgeway, Margaret, 107
Ridgeway, Matthew B., 106-11, 114
  assumes NATO command, 131
Ridgeway, Virginia Ann, 107
Roosevelt, Franklin, 33, 64
Roosevelt, Theodore, 32
Rusk, Dean, 78
Russia
  background to Korean conflict,
    31-8
  U.N. Security Council, 37-8
Russo-Japanese War, 32

San Francisco
  United Nations conference, 36
Scott, Winfield
  dismissal compared with General
    MacArthur's, 116-17
Sebille, Louis J., 84
Seoul, South Korea
  capital, 36
  North Korea takes, June, 1950, 24
  U.N. forces recapture, Sept., 1950,
    76
  Chinese take, Jan., 1951, 110
  U.N. forces recapture, Mar., 1951,
    111
Shepherd, Lemuel C.
  quoted, 105
Sherman, Forrest, 63, 68
"Siberia Hill" (battle), 134
Sicily, 58
Sino-Japanese War, 32
Slogans, quotations, and famous
    phrases
  "Drive carefully! The man you
    hit may be your relief!", 130
  "Home by Christmas", 79
  "I shall return!", 66
  Marine Corps Hymn, comic verse,
    87
  "Mr. Truman's War", 112
  "Only fourteen more shooting
    days until Christmas", 105
  "Why We Are Here" (text),
    109-10
Smith, Charles B., 25
Smith, Oliver, 90-2, 99
South Korea
  army, 24-6, 41, 57
  casualties, 41; of prisoners, 145
  map, 18
  Republic of Korea established, 36
"Squareheads", 86
"Stand-or-die" order, 46
Stevenson, Adlai, 131

Stratemeyer, George E.
  quoted, 85
Struble, Arthur, 70-2, 75

Taegu, South Korea, 53, 58-9
Taejon, South Korea
  North Korea takes, 26-7
  provisional capital, 25
Tanks
  attack Task Force Smith, 26
  Masan defense, 58
  Pusan beachhead, 52
Task Force Kean, 58
Task Force Smith, 25-6
"T-Bone Hill" (battle), 134
38th parallel
  Korean peace settlement after
    World War II, 34-5
  North Koreans cross, 20, 24
  North Koreans pushed back by
    U.N. forces, 77
  second Communist crossing, 106
Toktong Pass, 92, 94, 96, 98
Tokyo, Japan
  U.N. conference, 67
Treaty of Portsmouth, 32
Truce talks
  Kaesong, 122
  Panmunjom, 125, 128, 131
Truman, Harry S.
  argues with, fires General Mac-
    Arthur, 111-18
  General MacArthur and, 39, 79
  "police action" in Korea, 51
  reacts to invasion of South Korea,
    38, 39
Turkey
  casualties, 42
  combat forces, 41
Turncoats, 146

Underground fortresses, 126-7

United Nations
  brands China "aggressor", 110-11
  casualties, 41-2
  combat forces, 39, 41, 57, 70, 90
  founded, 35-6
  Korean peace settlement after
    World War II, 35
  reacts to invasion of South Korea,
    37-9

Valor awards, 148
Vance, Cyrus R.
  quoted, 148
Van Fleet, James, 119-25
  named Commander of 8th Army,
    114
  retires, 141
Van Fleet, James, Jr., 120
Voluntary repatriation, 131, 133,
    134, 142, 145

Walker, Caroline, 48
Walker, Sam Sims, 48
Walker, Walton, 45-52
  death, 51, 106
  General Dean and, 24
  General MacArthur and, 60-1, 86
  headquarters at Taegu, 53
  Frozen Chosen, battle, 90-105
Walmsley, John S., Jr., 84
Wasson, Marvin, 103
Williams, Sam, 42
Wolmi-do (island), 67-8, 69, 71-2
Wonsan, North Korea, 86-7

Yalu River
  Chinese Communists cross, 81
  U.N. forces forbidden to cross,
    85, 111
Yonghung-do (island), 69
Yudam-ni, North Korea, 90, 92
"Young Men's Association", 69